Better Eight Than Never

The MacLeod Siblings

Fly By Night Publishing

To Mom & Dad on their 40th Wedding Anniversary:

Thank you for taking care of us all these years. Through the good, bad, and everything in between we love you.

1

Jen

The Good: Grandparents

I've spent a lot of time thinking that those of us on the older end of the sibling spectrum had a different experience growing up. Sometimes that afforded us a bit more responsibility, and sometimes it permitted a bit more independence. But the one thing that I felt really stood apart for me was the way we were able to have relationships with our living grandparents.

Grandma April, Mom's mother, shared her appreciation of art, music, and so much more. She valued creativity in a way that I often think about and hope that I can convey to Connor. She did craft shows and shared her passion for her art media of the moment with us older grandchildren.

I remember "helping" her dye silk scarves in her big liquid vats, spinning wool with her, piecing quilts, and weaving. I remember when she purchased my first "real" set of paints. She spent the whole drive home from the craft store asking me to look at shadows on trees in order to see that color was everywhere, and that I shouldn't ever need to use black paint because that color does not exist in nature. Now, if only she had perhaps spent as much time on my technique on that first painting... gosh... that thing was hideous. But her lessons were things that echoed later on when I was enrolled in "real" art classes in college. Perhaps her desire to always find a way to have her art earn money inspired early thoughts on a career that permitted creativity and design.

She supported my first real foray into earning money through craft and my first venture into a real business the summer after we moved to Grand Forks. I would purchase and dress up bears in lace and hats. I'd go door to door selling them around the neighborhood, and I, to this day, still can't believe people actually purchased them. I like to think somewhere there's a little lace covered teddy bear sitting on top of a shelf in someone's home that someone purchased from a kid with a wagon that grandma helped me create.

My memories of Nana Hazel, Dad's Mom, or just "Hazel" as we were allowed to call her, in retrospect, provided a child led fun learning environment. She really didn't seem to care too much what we did, so long as we were safe and happy. She let us do terrible things, now in retrospect, that I'm sure made awful messes.

I remember making costumes out of sheets, using scissors, being equipped and permitted to bathe and scissor cut her Old English Sheepdog, Shabby, pretty much anytime we wanted to, permitted us to have ketchup packets in the car on trips, and more.

One of my most frequent memories that comes up most constantly is baking pies. We made pies everywhere, at her house, at our house, traveling, at the King & Prince at Christmas, and more. At her house she had a big wooden table. I remember that we would just scatter flour all over the table to make a work area, and she'd set us up with our own little bowl of flour, cold butter, and water, and we'd press it all together with our hands. If we wanted to roll the dough out she'd have us use our glasses (once we'd emptied them) and just roll it on top. We'd make some awful looking patchwork pies, but they always tasted good.

She always let us use the scraps at the end to make extra pieces of things—oftentimes we'd fill them with leftover filling and those darn things would expand when baked ultimately becoming one gooey mess with the pan that you'd have to flake off with a spatula. Love was that pie.

Papa Chuck never went by such a formal name to us. He was just "Papa." As a kid, I always envisioned Papa as a complete wild child stuck in an adult body. He was the fun one. The one that would do flips and belly flops off the backyard diving board. He had the best laugh and loved telling cheesy jokes. He would peel an orange leaving the peel all in one piece. He would take us on secret trips to Dairy Queen or Taco Bell. He also had an amazing woodshop that he built over his garage in the house in Augusta, GA.

When Dad was going through the tools he brought back from papa's shop, I only really had a craving for one tool. I'm sure it has a technical name but I knew it as the wood chisel. It was a small electric carving tool that Papa would set us up with in his shop. We would draw on a piece of scrap board and then chisel out our design. We spent hours in that shop with him sometimes... and he'd turn us loose safely on tools.

I remember sanding a piece of wood on his little spinning sander until there was almost nothing left. He especially liked making toys. Back when you could advertise cigarettes, I used to pull the pages from Marlboro cigarette ads because they had horses—which I was obsessed with—and he would glue them to boards and make custom puzzles for us. I'm sure most of the toys are lost to time and multiple moves, but he made so many cars, train tracks, small wooden horses (with rotating legs and, of course, horses that had one hoof in the air—because that's the only way I'd ever let them be!).

One summer he made small boats for us out of 2x4s. He chiseled out small windows and bent metal to make a small anchor. He let us decorate them with markers, most of which soaked off when we played with them in the pool. I count myself lucky that I have one of those boats now in my bathroom for Connor.

2

The Bad: Moves, Schools, and Houses

Until we came to Grand Forks, we moved a lot. Heck, even after we came to Grand Forks, just to ease into moving there, we sort of moved again. Really, while the move for Mom and Dad out to Minot seemed shocking, I suppose on some level it was just a return to what seemed to be a dominant part of the early part of my life. I've moved with them from Greenville, SC where I was born, to Monroe, GA, to Statesboro, GA, to Grand Forks, ND, then temporarily to Augusta, GA, before starting school back up in North Dakota in January, and then they left me when they moved to Minot, ND. I'm really excited for them to now be moving back to Grand Forks!

I have memories of the move from Greenville. Vague, vague memories. But the trauma of the experience as a young kid makes me laugh. I remember we had a white house where we rented the second floor. It had a small balcony or window. My details are a bit fuzzy, but an opening of some kind. I remember furniture going out the balcony as I suppose it was the easiest way to go out. I don't remember it, but Mom tells me I started chucking stuff out that I didn't want to be forgotten.

As a child you don't think too much about the stressors of moving two thousand miles from Georgia to North Dakota. Just prior, I remember having a small spat with a group of friends. I remember threatening that I was so mad and that if they didn't become nicer that I was going to move to North Dakota. Back then I thought North Dakota was this exotic place. We had visited a few times since our Kerian cousins lived there. It took a long drive to get there, it had big open sky, and in my heart at the time I knew it was amazing. Somehow Mom and Dad must have heard this threat because it seemed weirdly coincidental (or perhaps I don't remember everything in the right order and they had discussed it) that we suddenly were moving to North Dakota.

There was a moving company that did ultimately come in to do the move, but we still had to go through items and collect and sort. I remember being amazed at the size of the moving truck—running up and down the empty truck. I also remember when they somehow got the blue station wagon INSIDE the truck, and then Mom and Dad stuffed it full of stuff (even though I don't think we were supposed to do that). I also remember that my Tasmanian Devil stuffed doll, along with EVERYTHING my child self thought was their whole world, got lost in the move. When I noticed several things were missing on the other side, I was informed that some stuff was lost in the move. I remember envisioning a large brown box sitting at the end of the driveway in Statesboro—as tall as a fridge—and wishing we could just drive back down there to get it. I've later learned that several things that were "lost in the move" were actually tossed, but I think I'm ok with it now.

3

The Ugly: Flood Memories

Oddly some of my best memories came from the flood of 1997, a time that was the most stressful for many.

We worked hard to uninvite the Red River from our living room. I remember our sandbag "party" where we had neighbors, friends, and strangers come to our back yard to pile on sandbags. I remember, as a 7th grader, at school being bussed out to area neighborhoods to stack sandbags. I have wildly amazing memories of volunteering at sandbag central to fill thousands of sandbags.

As a kid, the flood, as a disaster, was my first real time that I connected that what I did could help contribute to society in a positive way. When all our efforts failed, I remember loading all the hamsters, guinea pigs, dogs, and random belongings into the back of a friend's car to escape across town as the National Guard was "shutting down" our neighborhood. It seemed surreal then, when the next day we woke up early to quickly empty that friend's basement of belongings and quickly then had to evacuate from town as water bubbled up from the street drains.

As kids, we didn't really understand the magnitude of what happened to so many people that were in the process of losing their homes. I remember listening to the radio as people called in (because there was no internet or cell phones) to ask the announcer how much water was in their neighborhoods. The announcers would say it was the basement, main floor, and in the case of so many, they said that rooftops were underwater.

We weren't really sure at the time what our home looked like, but at that point we were more focused on the fact we were going to spend the summer at the Kerians and in Georgia. We split time between the Heymans and Grandma and Papa's house and had the summer of our lives as Mom and Dad worked daily on the house on Lincoln drive which had six feet of water on the main floor.

I appreciate their willingness to send us away so we could have a normal summer of fun in the pool, chilling at the library, or exploring the tree farm property as they toiled demolishing the house down to the studs. By the time we returned at the end of the summer, they were starting to put sheetrock back up. Dad had saved a project for us. We had clippers and pulled all the nails out of the walnut paneling so it could be refitted. It's the same paneling that followed us to the 83rd street house, and again to parts and pieces of furniture as leftovers when they moved to Minot.

I'm partially attached to some of that—but mostly because I remember the days of pulling nails through it, pressure washing, and refinishing it so it could go back into a home that we all loved.

4

Katie

The Good: Flower Power

High school was all about figuring myself out through self-expression. I spent a lot of time learning to sew my own clothes, shopping at thrift stores, and exploring what Walmart had to offer in the kids' section. One day, I was at a fabric store buying up random fabrics for my latest creation and I stumbled upon the flowers section. There I found clip-on flowers. The best place for them? On my sharpie-decorated Chuck Taylors, already beaten up to near non-survival levels.

I wore that flower for the final months of my senior year of high school. It accompanied me to movie nights, bowling, punk rock shows, and everything in between. It became a part of my mostly black and frayed outfits and something that people identified with me.

At graduation, I hunted down a brand new flower to wear on my shoe for the ceremony. The occasion called for dressing up which I respected. Plus I didn't want to take off the flower from my Chucks.

Before the ceremony, we were all gathered in the commons area along with the school board. Mom, who was on the school board, was also in the room. While waiting, Phil Meyer approached me and informed me that my flower was inappropriate and it needed to be removed from my dressy heels. I did so but was visibly upset. Mom walked over to me and asked me what was wrong. When I told her I was shocked to hear her say "what can he really do to you?" So, I clipped the flower up my sleeve underneath my gown and made the walk over to the gym. Right before we walked in the door I quickly clipped it to my flower and jumped into place for the procession.

Sitting at the front of the gym, I thought it was over. However, Mr. Meyer walked right up to me and told me to remove it immediately. I did not. After the ceremony, Mr. Meyer was overheard saying that there wouldn't be another flower fiasco like there was that year.

I was so excited and proud when years later, Bridget decided to follow in my footsteps and clip her own flower to her shoe at her graduation.

5

The Bad: Construction Woes

So much construction. As a kid, I got to watch the construction happen as opposed to having to participate in it. So, to this day, I have a fascination with watching tile get installed after watching Papa install it to the ground floor of the Lincoln Drive house.

The flood changed everything for everyone. As kids, we missed the brunt of the work by being sent down to Georgia to stay until the house was somewhat livable. After what was actually a very fun, relaxing part of the summer, we were sent back to North Dakota to get the house ready. Suddenly, I was expected to take part in pulling nails and other glorious jobs that were deemed safe for a 5th grader.

The jobs continued for the next few years and when it was finally nearing an end, we had to move again. The house we moved to was wonderful but it needed some construction. The most vivid memory I have of working on the 83rd street house was installing the wood floors upstairs. Line after line after line after line of wood went in, until all I could see were lines of wood in my vision at the end of the day. Another fun project was the staircase getting installed from the kitchen to the mess hall. The temporary stairs were a bit of a hazard but it was fun to jump from stair to rickety stair.

On top of working on the 83rd street house, we were trying to salvage as much as we could in materials from the Lincoln Drive house. My favorite memory is salvaging the built-in bookshelf from Mom and Dad's room. They took out the windows on the second floor and we maneuvered that shelf onto the roof of the patio. Half of us were told to hold the shelf in place while the other half of the group went down to catch this massive shelf flying at them from a story above their heads.

All the materials were used in different ways. The former wood paneling was turned into a library and the kitchen cabinets from the old house were installed in the new kitchen. Wallpaper was picked out, new walls went up in the downstairs room to create bedrooms out of what was once a den. I still love the secret doorway between my and Ryan's room that we greatly underutilized.

Adventures aside, I'm just glad I don't wake up every Saturday with another project.

6

The Ugly: Road Trips

Road Trips. To most of my siblings they were something to look forward to. A funny story here, avoiding catastrophe there all while watching movies, reading, and sleeping. I have much different memories of these trips mixed in with all of the good and fun that was had.

My most memorable trip was on a camping trip to Glacier National Park. I had woken up some days before with a mild sore throat. I did the usual treatments but mildly swollen glands turned into a swollen throat. My diet consisted of water and applesauce because that's all I felt safe consuming. Of course this was all a mystery, we weren't sure what was wrong. I was taken in to see a medical professional—I think it was a nurse practitioner, but I'm not sure—and that professional tested me for mono and strep throat. As I opened my mouth for what I assume was an examination or a throat culture, the professional leaned in and then immediately jumped back in surprise. "I've never seen a throat this bad before!" she exclaimed. Needless to say, I was not reassured that my condition wasn't serious. Tests came back, negative for mono and strep.

Around that time, discussions were being had about what to do with me. The trip was happening but the question was, can Katie handle it? The answer was yes and away I went, sick as a dog, despite my protests that my friend's Mom would clearly love to take care of me for a week on short notice. I do understand the position that was taken, and hey what's a road trip without a good story?

We bounced around the road on the long drive to Glacier. I'm also blessed with car sickness so the journey was not exactly pleasant. I did have the luxury of two whole seats next to the tv! I'm sure I spent the entire trip complaining about how I felt, which was terrible.

We arrived at the campsite and set up. Camping was also one of my least favorite activities, so I was sick and grumpy all together. After a few days, my mystery illness cleared up and I was happy at the thought of eating solid food again. Often, at the end of a camping trip my parents would take us to eat a nice meal at a lodge. Considering I had gone a couple of weeks without eating solid food, I was determined to make the best of it. I can't remember what I ordered, I just remember eating everything on my plate. Now, one thing I was not aware of is that if you don't eat rich foods for a while and all of a sudden you gorge yourself, you will live to regret it. Which I definitely did.

7

Ryan

The Good: The Journey to Eagle, or Basic Training

My father is a proud man, and rightly so; his personal and professional accomplishments are truly legion. When he identifies a goal, he will walk through walls to accomplish it, self-reliant to an almost comical degree. This self-reliance and drive was, as far as I can figure out, the result of a combination of upbringing & family culture, combined with the tragic death of my grandfather when my father was only eighteen. My father found himself the oldest and most adult of his siblings, and had to create his life without his father's support.

He brought that self-reliance and pride in accomplishment to his parenting style, and encouraged our accomplishments as well, especially when those accomplishments built character. He made a point of having "how to" and wilderness books around at all times, along with a full library of classic stories.

I started reading at a young age, relentlessly. My first memories of literature are of my father reading The Chronicles of Narnia to us, one chapter at a time, each evening before we went to bed. On Sundays I would read the comics page of the paper, and very nearly understood

Dilbert & Doonsbury jokes (I'm pretty sure Dilbert is about a dog that thinks he's a person, it's basically "Family Guy" for the 90s). I continued to devour every book I could find. I read The Hobbit in first grade, and started reading the Bible in second, and read everything I could find by Robert Louis Stevenson, Mark Twain, and Jules Verne. I specifically remember reading Huckleberry Finn in Kindergarten, and completely missed that the story was about racism, not about a young boy with a dream of freedom escaping on a raft. Wanting to emulate Huck, I picked up the American Boy's Handy book and began to play at being Huck (when I wasn't being Peter Pan). My father saw the opportunity, and asked if I wanted to be an Eagle Scout. He explained that an Eagle Scout could navigate by the stars (just like Jim Hawkins from Treasure Island!), could build a shelter out of sticks, and could start a fire with only two matches. Clearly, if I wanted to be Huck, Peter Pan, Jim Hawkins, and the other adventurers of my stories, the first step was to become an Eagle Scout; fortunately, I had the best guide ever in my Eagle Scout father.

Having set my goal, I enrolled in tiger cubs at my school. We did all the standard cub scout things, we learned how to tie knots, how to build rockets, and how to fire guns (the adults who supervise groups of six-year-olds wielding firearms are far, far braver than I am). I worked hard, and my father was there every step of the way. I worked my way through the achievement ladder until I earned my Arrow of Light award, which allowed me to join Boy Scouts, for real, at age ten, instead of having to wait until I was an old man of eleven. I finished the first four ranks in the minimum time, while railing constantly against the existence of a minimum time requirement. My drive carried me through Star Scout by the time I was eleven, then Life Scout by age twelve. And then I hit a wall, which is when Dear Old Dad stepped in. He kept pushing me, kept driving me to meetings, and refused to let me quit even as I went to every length to avoid going. I had begun to feel the social pressures associated with scouting: it is an outdated group, only losers go to Boy Scouts, and the other hurtful things people use to keep anyone around them from achieving something they themselves lack the drive to achieve. This, too, is a lesson from Scouting and from my father: to push yourself to do great things and to leave behind anyone or anything standing in your way; to find a goal and work relentlessly toward it, breaking down walls to accomplish it. Finally, I was ready for my Eagle Project.

For those who don't know, what distinguishes an Eagle Scout from a Boy Scout is the completion of the Eagle Scout Project, which involves identifying, organizing, executing, and documenting a service project in your community. I found mine at a local heritage center meeting: one of their revenue sources is hay rides around the heritage village, and several of their wagons had been destroyed by a recent wind storm. It took all of the skills I had learned as a scout and as a bookworm: I raised funds, I bought supplies, I recruited volunteers, and I designed the wagon using a very advanced design program called "Microsoft Word".

But, if I'm being honest, none of that is true. I didn't do any of it; left to my own devices, I would have quit scouting entirely at age thirteen. When it came time to complete the project, I needed a roadmap, which my Dad provided. He advised me on direct solicitation of funds, and suggested corporate sponsors and experienced carpenters who could help me to do it. He, together with my Scoutmaster, helped me to persuade my fellow scouts to help me build it. When it was all completed, it would be nearly a year before I finished the report, which I finished with only a few weeks to spare before my eighteenth birthday—the end of the line. Even with the deadline approaching, I did no work on the project.

Enter Dear Old Dad. He sat me down and talked about the effort so far, about how the true lesson from Boy Scouts, the lesson he wanted me to learn, was the importance of finishing what you start. Ending my high school career with a completed achievement of the magnitude of Eagle Scout, that represented in a single sentence all of the knowledge I had gained, experiences that I had had, and the relationships I had made, set me up for a lifetime of stubbornly sticking to my convictions to the point of absurdity, and willingness to leave behind anything that stood in my way. Like father, like son.

I would not have completed the project if it weren't for Dad. I would not have learned self reliance, or the importance of teamwork, or how to lead a gang of unruly brats to actually accomplish something. I would not have been anything like the man I am today, if my Dad hadn't believed in me.

Even when I explicitly told him to stop.

8

The Bad: The Battle of Ragnarok (Online)

Don't think that I was the perfect child (far from it), I could fill an entire book with my exploits. I took Calvin & Hobbes as a guidebook for how to be a proper child; if you're not familiar with the comic series, stop reading this immediately, buy the boxed set, and read it cover to cover. You'll thank me.

Anyway, back to important topics: Me!

When I was sixteen, I had something of a rebellious streak (I know, sixteen-year-olds are normally so well-behaved and well-adjusted). I was particularly interested in the concept of authority and personal freedom, and especially scorned the idea of anyone with authority over me; this was a problem, because I was sixteen and I had two stressed-out parents who needed me to pretty much stay in line.

But I'm getting ahead of myself, I need to provide a disclaimer and give some backstory: The events of this story were extremely beneficial to me; I faced challenges and had to find new ways to attack problems, I gained skills and resilience that continues to help me in my daily life today. While I may regret the methods through which the skills were obtained, the life experiences outweighed the personal hardships (although I can't speak for the effect of my actions on others).

Now for the backstory: For my birthday the year before, I had been gifted the components of a computer by my mother, who had been playing with computers as a hobby for most of her adult life. She helped me assemble it and get it going, and I was ecstatic. I set about learning all that I could about computers, which is to say, just enough to be dangerous; most of my knowledge was hardware based, and I could hook anything up to anything else and make it do something (even if it wasn't what I intended for it to do).

Just before my sixteenth birthday, I discovered online role-playing games; specifically, an animated Japanese thing called Ragnarok Online. For those who don't know me, I have an immersive personality: When I discover a new subject of interest, I dive in headfirst and don't come up for air until I have exhausted every element of knowledge, joy, and understanding left in the subject; this works great for things like Geometry, but not so well for massively-multiplayer sandbox games with literally limitless activities.

We had dial-up internet, which for those who don't know is an archaic way of accessing computer networks through the phone line. It was slow, loud (Best attempt at explaining the noise while it connected: SKRRREEEEoooWEEEEoooWEEEEOOOWEEEEbzzzzbzzbzzz), and took up the phone line while you were using it. Partly because it prevented calls from coming through, but also because continuous access to the internet is maybe not something that children should have access to (please be careful on Google), we had a limitation on how much time we spent on the computer/internet after school; you'll notice where I put the emphasis in that rule.

Enter rebellious, anti-authority Ryan, who loved to find ways around problems and fantasized that he was a tech guru from the movies who could hack into anything and had just discovered a fun new game with lots to learn about, that rewarded continuous play and charged a monthly subscription.

The monthly subscription was a key part of what happened next. I had begun to understand finance, and this seemed like a straightforward calculation: If it costs me $10/month to play as much as I want, and I play for one hour, then it costs me $10/hr to play the game. If, on the other hand, I played for 160 hours (actual playtime numbers from the month of March that year), then it only costs me six cents an hour! I had discovered a backdoor hack into the clever ponzi scheme that was Ragnarok Online.

An online subscription that rewarded excess gaming, a completionist drive to pull all value from anything that interested me, an internet connection that prevented phone calls, a basic understanding of computer and network hardware, a drive for freedom and fairness, and a legalistic understanding of rules created a perfect storm of adolescent anti-establishment feeding frenzy.

The rule, I will remind you, was that our internet use was limited after school. It was worded this way deliberately to encourage us to get up early and get ready in the mornings; having made the assumption that they were dealing with rational and sane people, my parents thought it would work well.

I began testing the limits: I first got up at 5 AM, then 4, then 2, then midnight. I would arrive home from school at 4 PM, go to bed immediately, and wake up six hours later at 10 PM to log onto the game. I played on weekends. I played at school (turns out school firewalls are pretty easy to get around, but that's another story). It was a full-blown addiction, and I loved it. My parents, being generally caring people, did not.

So they changed the rule; we could no longer play before 5 AM. Just to be certain that they were covered, they installed a parental control program that restricted our online hours to between 5 AM and 10 PM, and limited us to an hour per day (cruelty!). That should have been the end of it, but remember that I was a sixteen-year-old that did not like authority, and especially didn't like when authority changes the deal when they don't like the outcome. As far as I was concerned, by changing the rule my parents had broken our agreement. This was War.

This seems like a good spot for an interlude, during which I would like to remind you that this is the "Bad" story, not the "Ugly" one. Anyway, back to the narrative.

The parental control program was my first challenge. The administrator account was on my Mom's computer profile, which was protected by a password; the program itself was protected by a different password. Fortunately for me, I was a sponge for information, and I had picked up on some of my parents password themes; I found a reason to ask for my Mom to make an adjustment, which required her to enter her password, and I looked over her shoulder to reduce the list of available options and brute-forced my way into her profile after that. I changed my time restrictions to force me to log out at 10 PM, but then allow me back on at midnight instead of 5 AM. I got rid of the hour restriction, but got to practice self-control and limit myself to an hour a day while my parents were awake (see, character-building made it into the story!).

    My parents had neglected a reality: They needed to sleep; I had just finished proving that I did not, and technically speaking I wasn't breaking any rules by continuing to sleep from 4PM-10PM. I started sleeping in until midnight, well after my parents went to sleep, and logging on then. My parents started to check if I was online late at night; remember, this was dial-up internet, and picking up the phone revealed a tell-tale "SKREEEEEEEE" noise that was a pretty dead giveaway. My Mom would pick up the phone in her room, and leave it off the hook if she heard me on the internet.

    This was, of course, unacceptable. I tried waiting until she went back to sleep, then snuck into their room to hang up the phone; that worked exactly one time. I needed something more permanent; that's when inspiration struck. A network is essentially just a large circuit, and any element within a circuit can be bypassed. So I grabbed my wire cutters and electrical tape, cut the phone cord to their room, and spliced it into my room to complete my circuit while leaving them out. I could use the internet, they couldn't interrupt me, and everyone was happy.

    This naturally escalated the problem. There was nothing that my parents could do about my ability to splice the network; I knew where the cords were and moving or protecting them was prohibitively difficult. Next level of defense: The internet password! Easy enough to change, so they reset it; now we had to ask permission every time we got onto the internet. Here's where I got to practice my deception and persuasion skills, as well as make use of that password detector that I was talking about. I asked my Dad to log me onto the internet, and deployed my detector to find the password. This worked several times before they caught on, probably when they got a call from the school that I was sleeping through social studies (to be fair, when am I ever going to use geography in real life?).

So they tried another route: My beloved computer, which I had built myself, had to be removed from my room and put in the "Mess Hall", which was what we called the hallway-room that served as a sort of hub for our house; it was visible from my parents room. Now it was my turn to secure a computer system; this was now about survival!

I became obsessed with computer security; I locked down my computer so tight that Neo himself would have plugged right back into The Matrix. I had passwords on everything, I put a padlock on the case, and a bike chain attaching the whole thing to my desk. I changed my password weekly, then daily; I developed passwords that I have continued to use to this day, passwords that could be very clearly hinted at but only if you knew about which life-experience I was referencing in my three layers of encryption. This was, of course, unnecessary in hindsight: no one cared what was on my computer, they just didn't want me using it to play excessive online games; I suppose that they were successful in that regard, because at this point I was spending too much time on computer and network security to care much about leveling up my wizard.

I no longer felt safe. If my parents could claim any piece of my property at any time based on how I was using it, was anything really "mine"? Could I actually claim anything as my own, or could they just decide arbitrarily that it "wasn't good for me" and take it away? All of my punishments and childhood confiscations came flooding forward to confirm this fear: If they can take away my computer, can they take my chair! My clothes! My microwave! So I barricaded my door closed and escaped through the window.

Escaped, that is, to the front door, so that I could go to school as normal. Before we get into this next part, I want to say I feel at least partially justified in barricading my door, because they never would have known it was barricaded if they hadn't been trying to go into my room without telling me.

But yeah, they found out that my door was blocked, so they sent in the big guns: five-year-old Bridget lowered herself into my window (it was a basement room) and cleared the barricade, allowing my parents (well, my Mom did most of the work, because Dad worked in the afternoons) to remove its components and, as punishment, my door.

To put it mildly, this did not sit well with me. I had a screwdriver, and I knew how to use it. This was going to be fun!

My first thought was to repay the injustice in kind: I removed my parents door and tried to fit it into my bedroom door frame. Unfortunately, it was much too large (another injustice, surely. I should have the biggest door!). Having done the work and not wanting to let the cleverness of my retaliation go to waste, I stashed the door in the back of my room (never said I was the brightest kid) and set about finding my original door. There were only a few places to stash a door: it wasn't in the barn, it wasn't in the garage, therefore it was locked in the basement closet five feet from my room. In retrospect, I probably should have checked there first.

I hadn't yet picked up lock picking, so I was stuck. Then, a realization hit me: I didn't need to unlock the door, I just needed to get past the door! So I leveraged my newfound knowledge of doors: They can be removed at the hinges. I popped the door off, grabbed my door back, and left the closet door in the middle of the hallway.

Here's where things get really crazy. I was reaching points of paranoia that bordered on the obscene, and I started to work out what their next moves might be. Remember the computer? Remember that I had learned that my property was not mine, and if they decided that I was using it incorrectly it could be forcibly taken? So I dismantled the computer, and locked it in the giant locked chest in Scott's room, whose combination we had all forgotten years ago. Here's the secret: Locks don't work if you have a screwdriver to take off the hinges.

When my Dad got home, pardon the language but there is no other way to express it: $#!+ hit the F*&7!ng fan. He demanded to know how it is that I felt that I had the right to damage his property; for some reason, the irony wasn't as clear as I had hoped, apparently sixteen-year-olds don't have the best understanding of the nuances of social rules.

I'm sort of proud of the fact that I predicted the computer thing: My computer was to be confiscated and returned to Mom's hobby collection, which is to say likely cannibalized. They went to get it, but it wasn't there. I was threatened with grounding, full house arrest, camps for errant boys, everything and the kitchen sink to get me to reveal the location of the computer, but I didn't budge.

So they emptied my room. Like, literally, emptied it. I had clothes in a drawer on the floor and a mattress on the floor. I did get to keep my door though, they realized that there was nowhere that I couldn't get, so there was no point confiscating the door again. And I got to keep my computer, although I couldn't use it until I went to college. So we'll call that one a stalemate.

And there you have it. The epic story of how a deluded sixteen-year-old, in a desperate attempt to play a video game, learned to tamper with computer & network hardware, learned low-level software hacking, and adaptively problem solved to achieve his admittedly deluded goal; which, by the way, he forgot about halfway through (Ragnarok Online? No?).

There's a moral in here somewhere, but I'm not sure what it is. I'm open to suggestions!

9

The Ugly: The War of the Cherries

I have no allergies, of which I am aware. I frequently get hay fever during pollen season, but I've learned to manage it, and the sun and I have come to an understanding. I get poison ivy and a raised bump from mosquito bites. Nothing serious.

In this story, we're going to learn about the night that I learned that I was deathly allergic to: cherries. Specifically, cherry pie. The kind of cherry pie that is served at a big medical convention to doctors who listen to lectures on something entirely too boring for a six-year-old to pay attention to.

From an early age, Mom and Dad drilled good table manners into us. It was very important that everyone knew how to conduct themselves at a formal dinner. It was our task to set the table, and we learned to do it properly. We learned to keep our elbows down, and that "Tables are made for cups and glasses, not for a little boy's feet or...Ryan, get off the table." I never understood why the adults all laughed whenever someone said that, but there was always a vague sense that they were laughing at you, so you learned pretty quickly to stay off the table.

Importantly, we learned how to eat politely. Coil or cut your noodles, never put more on your fork than you can eat in one bite, chew with your mouth closed, swallow before you speak, and never put more than one bite in at once. NEVER pick up a bowl of soup and drink it like hot cocoa. We were frequently offered opportunities to practice out at the Royal Fork, a local buffet. If we behaved ourselves well, we were rewarded with unsupervised dessert time during which we had full access to all of the jello, pudding, and ice cream we could stomach. Failure to properly behave meant you had to sit by the adults until they finished their conversation, which was invariably the most boring thing ever conceived. Needless to say, we learned quickly how we should behave.

As a result of this training, Mom and Dad were able to take us out sometimes to REALLY fancy places. We've gone to Papa's country club, we've eaten oysters at fine restaurants with views of Lake Superior, we've accompanied our parents to weddings and convention dinners, and we generally (mostly) behaved well enough that our parents didn't have to rush us out of the room (sorry Mom).

This particular incident was some kind of convention hall at a hotel thing, so I'm reasonably certain that it was at one of my Dad's doctors' conventions. I think that we had spent the day out on the town with Mom, because I don't remember any of the normal convention trappings, but I do remember the dinner.

We got dressed up nice, and we were served dinner as someone at the front droned on about something to do with something boring. I think the meal was steak or fancy chicken or fish; it always was at fancy dinners, which makes it difficult to remember this particular food. The dessert though, the dessert I remember. Sweet, delicious, juicy cherry pie, with sparkling sugar crystals on top and an enormous whipped cream dispenser. I had been trained for this.

Having been promised dessert, I had behaved myself through dinner. They brought the pie out, and I politely waited my turn at the table. I politely waited my turn and politely ate the first slice of pie while sitting politely at the table. Then the adults lost interest, and the buffet table was just. Right. There.

So I grabbed a couple more slices. I started to feel queasy, so I figured the obvious reason must have been that I was hungry, so I ate two more. I was really feeling sick, so I thought I should just find somewhere quiet to lie down...somewhere like under the buffet table. That way I had easy access to more pie.

My memory gets hazy here, but I remember being found under the table lying in a pool of bright red vomit. My Dad, the doctor, was of course horrified; partly because I had ruined the carpet in the convention hall, but mostly because it looked like I was vomiting blood, which is never good.

They brought me home, and I was sick the rest of the evening. I'm pretty sure that I was legitimately sick, like with the flu, and the cherries had just sped up the process a little, but once you see a full pie's worth of cherries in reverse, it sort of turns you off to cherries for a while.

I decided that I must be allergic to cherries. My Dad tried to convince me that cherries are not a known allergen, but that only proved that I was a unique case! The first in the world, someone should write a medical paper on me! I didn't eat cherries until prom, when I found out that there were cherries in Shirley Temples (after I'd enjoyed a few dozen). But that's another story...

10

Scott

The Good: What Doesn't Kill You Makes You Stronger

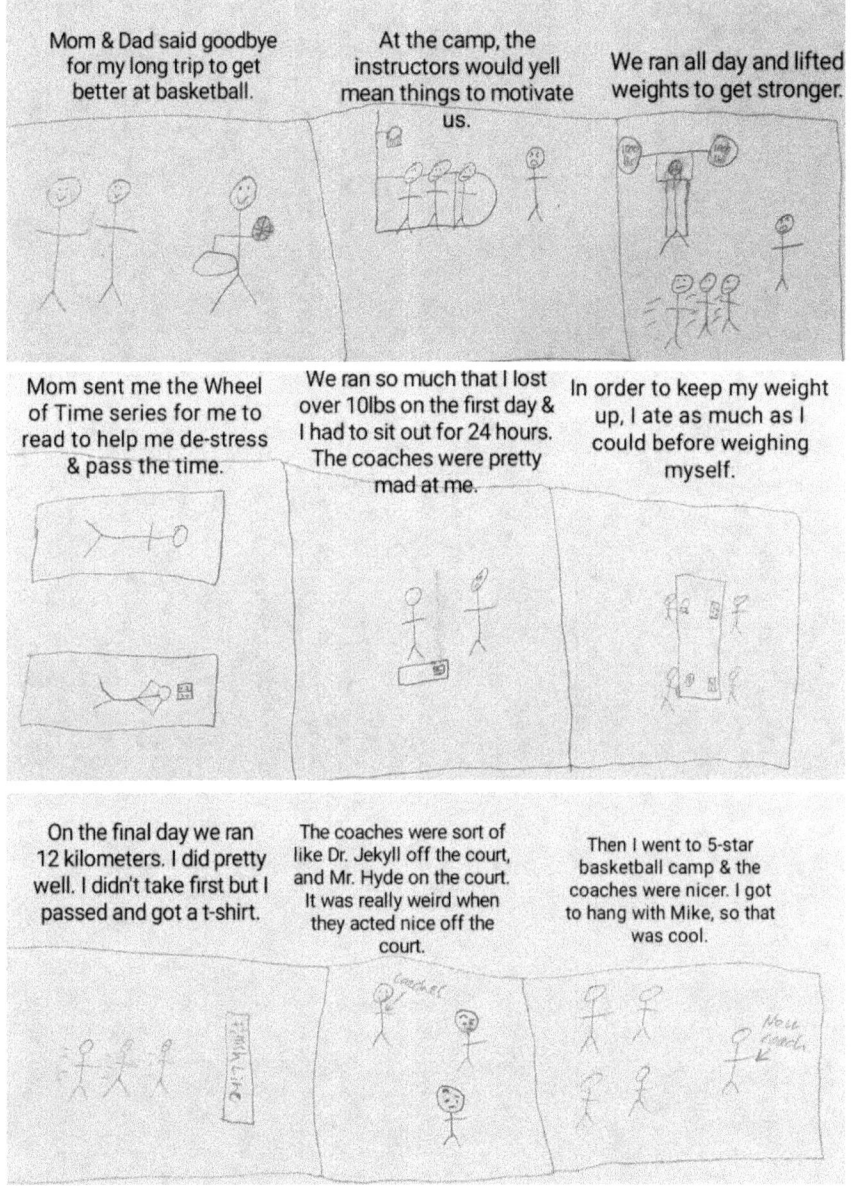

The Bad: Did You Hear the Thunder?

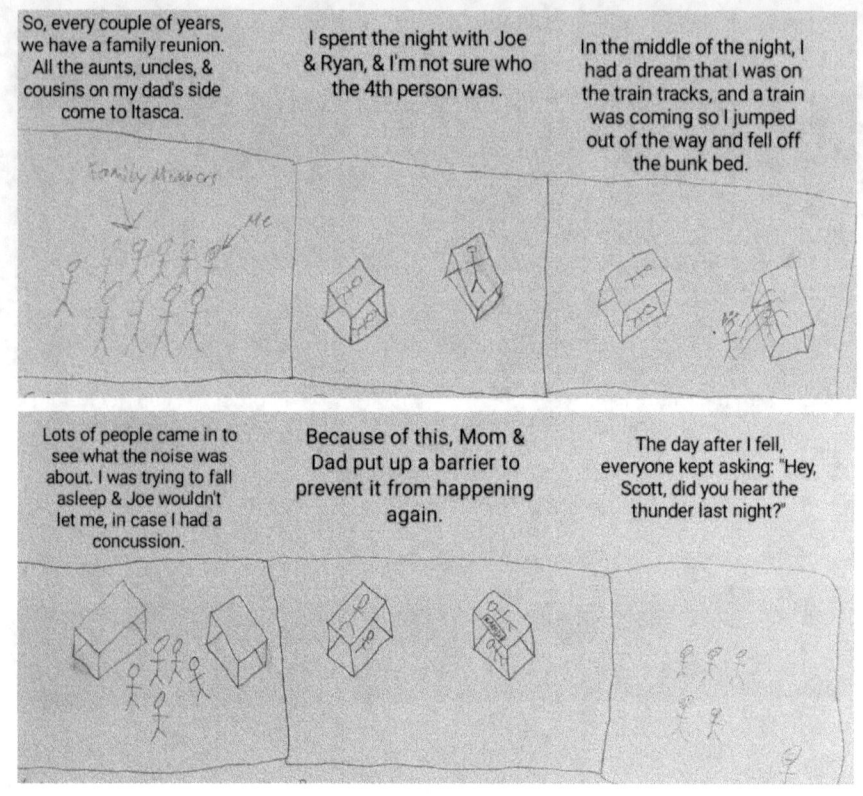

The Ugly: The Source of My Abandonment Issues

One night, we were on a road trip & needed gas, so we stopped at a run down gas station.

I was still awake, and needed to use the restroom, so I stepped out without telling anyone.

Mom & Dad finished filling up & got back in the van.

I got done using the bathroom and saw they were leaving!

Mom & Dad said they were driving & heard knocking/banging on the car. They stopped and discovered I was the one making the noise.

11

Brett

The Good: Family Car Trips

The destination does not matter. What matters is the journey. But also, the destination is pretty important. I mean, it is the whole reason for the journey. So, really, reverse that and we have a profound saying. Anyway, here is a story about the journey.

The MacLeod road trip is a thing of legend and pride. Stubbornly, we would spurn purchasing ten plane tickets and would opt instead for an odyssey across the country. Many people would not look fondly on living out of a car for multiple days, even weeks with nine other people, roaming to a different town every night, and eating whatever you could scrounge up that your older, crueler siblings left behind for you. But I look back fondly on the experience as formative. And, as Calvin's father would say, "it builds character".

I think fondly on these experiences and mark them "good", because they are some of the longest periods the entire family was forced to be together. We were forced to cooperate regarding entertainment. And as everyone knows, Pete's Dragon is the epitome of entertainment.

We formed an efficient ring of snack distribution that was fair, and not at all abused by whomever happened to be nearest the snack cooler. In fact, I remember fondly that each of my younger sisters would opt for their own can of soda, an "adult" beverage only to be had on special occasions but were unable to finish their drinks. Generously, I would offer to finish them for them, securing in addition to my own full can, another one and a half sodas. This occurred every time we were offered a soda. Yes, fair and unabused the system was.

As for entertainment, I still brag today about our multi-screen system with complete in car entertainment center that was set up by our mother. It was fairly advanced and will likely not be seen again since the dawn of tablets and embedded TVs has rendered the setup obsolete. With this system we could watch any VHS, or eventually DVD, that the family owned. Each row of seats had their own screen, preventing anyone from blocking their view.

So naturally, with this setup, everyone opted to watch Pete's Dragon on repeat. Occasionally, other films and shows would make their way into rotation. I remember developing a love for Hogan's Heroes and Gilligan's Island and likely would not have seen these masterpieces otherwise.

We were also able to adapt the system to plug our Xbox gaming system and play games as we traversed the country. This technique certainly was ahead of its time and as yet there is no suitable way to play graphically intense games in the vehicle without a system similar to ours. Unfortunately, as the consoles became more power intensive, they were unable to run from the car battery. This effectively made gaming in the car impossible. We now await the day that cloud gaming becomes accessible enough to bring us back to where we were twenty years ago.

And of course, there were many sights to see along the way. During our escapades we would stop at countless parks, monuments, campgrounds, hiking trails, museums, or other significant areas, sometimes even family. We are likely one of the most well-traveled families. And when I say that, I mean one that has stopped at all the stops between here and Florida and seen all there is to see within drivable distance. In fact, I believe we may have the record for most pictures of park signs taken.

Often people will take the plane to get them to their destination faster, but as was stated in the beginning of this rambling, it is the destinations along the journey, not the journey nor the destination. Or something like that. I'm not a philosopher.

12

The Bad: Middle Mischief

Being the youngest of three boys it clearly became a mission to cause as much havoc and destruction as possible, in general, making Dad's life more difficult. There is a compilation of things we did together that inevitably ended in harm or destruction. Chiefly among these, I remember how amazing it was that you could take an ordinary kitchen knife and let it drop into the floor.

If you did this properly the knife would stick straight up just like the movies! I remember doing this constantly without a care for the damage we were doing to the floor or the knives themselves. It was cool, it was fun, it was worth doing. I am not sure if we were ever caught or found out, but it would have been worth it anyway.

I also remember in the kitchen clambering up the counter to retrieve something rudely stored higher than I could reach at the time. Being the embodiment of dexterity, I expertly stood upon an open cabinet door to reach my goal. Through factors unbeknownst to me, I slipped and came crashing down straddling the lower cabinet, ripping it from its hinges. I believe that I did not get away with that particular endeavor.

Another time my brothers and I were planning to create a pool in our front yard. The process was simple, we would dig a hole and fill it with water. After all, that is all a pool is. And why would we want to use the pool in our house when we could have a second in the front yard?

Of course, the process went about as well as you would expect it. We made an excellent hole in the ground and began filling it with water. Promptly the hole turned into mud. Persistent as we were, we made use of the pool anyway. It went swimmingly, until we emerged covered neck to toe caked in mud. We received enormous amounts of sympathy from our family as they took pictures before hosing us off with cold water. The hole itself collapsed shortly thereafter.

My father always purchases fireworks on the days after Independence Day, for a discount, then stores them year-round. This is likely the more frugal method of fireworks purchasing, unless your sons get into the stash and use Boy Scout ingenuity to light the fuses with magnifying glasses. It worked amazingly well. To this day I have no idea how none of us got hurt and how nobody came yelling from the house, but we launched many fireworks and even held the cannons against our chests to angle them where we wanted, as though we were launching a real cannon. As I said, nobody was hurt, but the damage here was the many fireworks we wasted. It was really an excellent show though, if put on by amateurs.

The last day I played baseball I remember clearly. My older brother Scott wanted to practice his pitching. Being the helpful brother I was, I decided to catch for him. After a few pitches I missed the catch, and of course was not wearing any safety gear. The ball went right into my eye. Having learned a bit about medicine since then I now realize how lucky I am that I did not burst my eyeball or fracture my skull. Of course, these things were checked by CT scan, and even though I was miraculously okay, I was not able to see through the swelling for at least a week.

For some reason, as a child, I liked to put things in odd places and forget them there. I do not know the reasoning behind this or what enjoyment I got from it, but it happened. Two times in particular it resulted in damage. Once I stored a pen in the bottom of the oven. This made sense to me at the time. Naturally, when the oven was next used, the pen heated, melted, then superheated ink spread throughout the bottom of the oven. My mother was pleased.

Another time I was very safely playing with a razor blade. I dropped that one in the back of our La-Z-Boy and left it alone, figuring it lost forever to the void of the recliner. I will not tell the result of that story, as that one belongs to Erin, but suffice it to say, Erin was the one who found it later.

13

The Ugly: Philmont

Philmont was that surprise mixture of good and bad. There is no word for it but ugly. But even still, you can love something ugly.

Philmont is a summer hiking opportunity for Boy Scouts. We would abandon all of our worldly luxuries for two weeks to walk under the hot sun and pouring rain carrying everything on our backs. Yes, it was miserable. Yes, we loved it. It is truly amazing, I can look back and remember how miserably hot, wet, sweaty, and tired I was, and still want to return to that experience. In some way, all of the pain and misery gets washed away and you only think of the amazing views, once in a lifetime experiences, and personal encounters with bears.

To understand Philmont, you have to know the basic rule. Everything outside of the base camp is trying to kill you. We soon found out how fundamentally true this is. Your first trek outside of the base camp you are full of hope and energy. That hope and energy becomes dashed immediately as soon as you realize there are five unmarked trails and you don't know which to take. You opt to look at the map and find yourself even more lost. The map is outside of base camp. The map is trying to kill you.

Somehow, we found the correct trail and made our way through the beautiful mountainside of New Mexico. Soon, however, we were beset upon by mini bears, the ferocious beasts that would steal your food, chew your water tubing, and in general make your life miserable. You could not let your guard down for a second lest one of these tiny monsters ruin your day. The mini bears are outside of basecamp. The mini bears are trying to kill you. We survived the mini bears by setting watches and ensuring nothing was left unguarded during our breaks.

Somehow, we only lost one Camelbak.

Water is a prized commodity in Philmont. The minimum amount you would drink each day was a gallon. To replenish our supplies, we were forced to fill our water from the local rivers. The river, however, is outside of base camp, therefore, the river is trying to kill you. There are innumerous bacteria in these river waters, not helped by the fact that Philmont is an active ranch and therefore, the multiple cow pies leak their contents into nearby rivers. To counter this, we would be forced to filter every drop we drank, or sterilize it with tablets which made the water taste horrendous and did nothing for the "chunks" floating in it. We drank at least a gallon of this water a day.

The sun itself is outside of base camp. The sun is trying to kill you. We would rise each morning well before dawn to beat the blasted sun to our next camp. As soon as you could see your feet, we were out of camp hiking to our next destination. Often, we were forced only a few hours under that brutal beating sun, covered in sunscreen multiple times over, hoping to avoid a burn that would rub the entirety of the trip. As daylight would crest over the trees we would sing "Here Comes the Sun", a song of warning and doom.

We had two further near encounters with death while hiking the trails.

At one point we came around a corner and found ourselves face to face with a bear. Now remember this bear is outside of base camp. This bear was trying to kill us. The group remained calmly panicked as we gathered into one large group, using all our Boy Scout knowledge. The bear was unfazed.

We began to sing songs at the bear in our out of tune way in hopes to drive it away much like anyone else that heard us sing. The bear was unfazed. Eventually we gave up trying to drive it off and sang loudly as we slowly moved around it. We successfully passed it as it was more interested in other things but continued to sing for a while in case more bears were around. We sang right as we rounded a corner and came face to face with another, greatly confused troop. The troop was frightened by our singing.

There are two great peaks in Philmont. One is mount Baldy, the other is the Tooth of Time. Amazingly, you can get lost on both trails up and still find your way to the peak. You need only look up, see the peak, and state to your fellow troop mates "that's where we're going".

This method worked well, and I highly recommend it to anyone climbing the peaks. Only a few times were we clambering, without any safety gear, over large gaps with 200 foot drops only steps to our left. A simple ascent. Getting down proved to be another matter, however. As we made our way to the peak we could look out and see the gorgeous view and incoming storm clouds.

For those unfamiliar with Philmont storms, they often come out of nowhere and are brutal in both rain and lightning. To get the warning that we did was in a way a saving grace. After seeing the incoming storm, we picked up and ran. The storm was outside of base camp. It was trying to kill us.

I am not exaggerating when I say I feared for my life at that Moment. We were sprinting along a ridge connecting two peaks, fully exposed and watching the lightning crash below us. There was no separation between the thunder and the lightning. And the thunder was so incredibly crushing you could feel it in your bones as the flash was blinding you. I am amazed that none of us were hit, and I cannot wait to return to Philmont to do it all over again.

14

Erin

The Good: Procrastination and Indiana Jones

As anyone who knew me as a child will attest, I've wanted to be a writer almost my whole life. I can't tell you how much printer paper I wasted as a four-year-old typing up my stories and then being very upset Mom wasn't reading what I'd written. She might've had an easier time of it if I'd bothered to learn to read or write first, but I was a precocious child.

Over the years, I occasionally dipped my toes in the writing world. I joined a young writers group, made three separate attempts at beginning a story, and even published some middle-school poetry. Fortunately, most of these early attempts have been lost to the sands of time or willfully destroyed.

It wasn't until my sophomore year of college that those dreams turned into something concrete and it was all because I'd told my choir friend (now best friend) Dani that'd I'd finished reading the story she'd sent me (I hadn't) and I just needed to finish writing down my critiques (I hadn't even started). She wanted to go over them with me, so I invited her back to my dorm room and told her about a story idea I had while I hurriedly read through and critiqued her work.

The story idea in question was inspired by a legend about the MacLeod family I'd read in a book my oldest sister, Jen, made for interim one year. In the legend, the MacLeod Chief marries a fairy woman and has a child with her. Her father forces her to leave her new family after a year and a day and she makes her husband promise to never let their son cry because she'd be able to hear it in fairyland. The chief is despondent after his wife leaves and his nobles throw a grand party to cheer him up, one that tempts the child's nurse to creep away to watch the festivities. The child kicks off his blanket and begins to cry but the nurse can't hear him over the music. His mother, far away in fairyland, can hear him though and she rushes to his nursery to comfort him, wrapping him in her shawl and singing a lullaby before fleeing again.

Wouldn't it be cool, I'd said, if that legend were true? If there were people alive today with the blood of fairies running through their veins? Could we somehow reverse engineer fairies through generational genetic engineering?

The idea didn't leave me. I've always loved the logistics of fantasy and this was turning into a smorgasbord. How would someone accomplish that? How would it affect modern society? What would it mean for someone if their child or their spouse suddenly became a fairy?

You'd think I'd start there then, but I didn't want to tell a story about the beginning of all this, I wanted to tell a story where the main character gets thrust right in the middle of a world that already grappled with these questions and found some answers.

Procrastination struck again and I wrote the prologue and first chapter to what became Haven while I was supposed to be working on homework for my computer class. I got through three more chapters before I realized I should hammer out some worldbuilding details and stopped writing new material while I worked out how, exactly, I was going to answer all my questions.

Honestly, this wasn't my first attempt to write a book and I'm not entirely certain my family thought I'd actually go through with it. If it hadn't been for Dani, I might not have.

It took six months and firmly establishing that I was a night owl who did my best work long after everyone else was asleep, but I did it. At three o'clock in the morning on June 10th, I finished my first draft of Haven. It was a 120,000 word mess, riddled with plot holes, grammar mistakes, and awkward writing and it was mine.

In the style of all young writers who'd just finished their first major work, I was convinced it was perfect and any publisher would kill for the rights to such a magnificent piece of fiction. The only thing that stopped me from sending it off to agents right then was the thought that I might have made a few grammar errors, so I thought I'd read through it once to find all the errors.

I found a lot of errors. So many, in fact, that I was beginning to think maybe this wasn't a masterpiece and I might need some help.

Thank heaven for that because I went looking for help. Perhaps scarred from all my previous writing attempts growing up, my siblings didn't care to read that first draft or were too polite to admit it was garbage, so I reached out to strangers on the internet and began the agonizing process of beating the crud out of something I'd poured my heart and soul into.

It hurt. A lot. I'm grown enough to admit that I didn't take my initial critique well at all. It was my readers who were the problem. They were the ones who couldn't see what I was doing, why these scenes needed to be just so and why I had to cover so much middle ground between the bits of action. Criticism felt like an attack against me and not genuine attempts to fix what was wrong with Haven.

But it was hard to admit there weren't faults. The beginning suffered from being written first, before I'd really caught my stride, and from being constantly rewritten while I worked. The middle was a slog, almost fifteen chapters where nothing much happened at all. It made me laugh while writing it, that my characters didn't make it to the eponymous haven until chapter ten and that my protagonist didn't meet the deuteragonist until over halfway through the book. The end was where things really picked up and I'd gotten a lot of compliments and swearing about my climactic scene, but many of my subplots didn't go anywhere and none of my characters really had any development at all.

After a year of work, I'd deleted the first 1.5 chapters, established the setting, and somehow managed to trim 5,000 words of garbage from the middle. I'd burned a lot of bridges doing so. It's hard enough to get strangers to read unedited garbage once, let alone two or three times while you fiddle with the tricky bits. Honestly, there's a part of me that wants to track down my early beta readers and apologize for making them deal with Haven before I'd accepted I needed to put the work in to make it better.

While I was complaining to Mom and Dad about how hard it was to find readers I didn't have to pay for, Dad agreed to read Haven if I'd print it out for him.

It took three hours, two cartridges of ink, and more swearing than I'll admit to as I manually turned each page over to get the printer to print double sided, but I managed it for him. It was an inch thick and barely fit in the binder I'd found, but seeing it physically like that made my stomach twist.

I'd done that. That whole story was the product of my work and one day I was going to see it on shelves everywhere.

The thing about Dad, which is a blessing and a curse, is that he's never really seen the point in pulling his punches. So when he read through Haven, he had a lot of thoughts. He pointed out my crutch words, some plot holes, the truly sloggy mess that was the middle, and that even though Haven was still 112,000 words long the only body language I had was an excessive amount of eye movements.

But his biggest contribution is something I'm not certain he'd remember if asked about it.

While I was editing one night, he decided to put on Indiana Jones and the Last Crusade, which I didn't mind. I wasn't making much progress and that's my favorite Indiana Jones movie.

About midway through the film, Sean Connery's character manages to take down a biplane by frightening a flock of seagulls into flying in front of it. It's one of my favorite scenes because it's ridiculous and it breaks up the drag of constant chase and fighting scenes that take up 80% of the movie.

Dad turns to me as Sean Connery is walking along the beach with his umbrella and says "You know what your book needs? A scene like that in the middle."

At the time, I laughed. It didn't make much sense to me. All my readers said the middle was already too long, what would I gain by making it even longer?

But it stuck with me. I watched the scene again and had to admit, it broke up the monotony of Harrison Ford punching people. It was funny and helped break the tension that had been building since Indy found out his Dad had been kidnapped.

It occurred to me that Dad wasn't saying I needed a funny scene like that, I just needed something different than my characters sitting in the back of a van, unable to affect the plot.

That was the turning point in my edits. Haven wasn't turning out the way I was expecting so why shouldn't I take the risk and change it like that? I wrote digitally so it wasn't like I couldn't go back if I didn't like it.

I wrote a scene where my main character's family is nearly caught and their saviors are partially at fault for it. It turned the slog into something nearly thrilling and gave my main character something to do besides pontificate at his children.

Now that I'd gotten rid of the idea that the story didn't have to stay exactly the same as I'd written it, it was like I'd been given permission to go wild.

I devoured craft books, purchased a body language handbook for writers, and brutally cut darlings that didn't move the plot along. In one draft, I managed to cut out a net 10,000 words between adding character development scenes, firming out the plot, and letting my characters interact with the world around them.

Haven was starting to read like an actual book and not something pounded out in a sleep-deprived haze by a college student with class in three hours.

I started offering to swap work with other writers I met in chat rooms and writing forums and my editing became even more brutal. I couldn't criticize someone for using epithets or for not using body language if I wasn't willing to correct those errors in my own writing. I met many wonderful writers in that time, some of whom I still read for today.

At a certain point, I had to admit I'd hit a wall. I'd been editing and revising Haven for three years and, while my readers loved it more with each draft, I knew it could be better. I just couldn't get it there on my own.

So I bit the bullet, saved for three months, and hired an editor. It cost a lot, especially for someone barely making enough to cover rent and suffering from a crippling unwillingness to cook, but it was worth it. This was an industry professional, someone who knew what she was talking about. If she said Haven was ready to start sending to agents, it was ready.

She liked it, but I couldn't get agents to look at it. Truth be told, Haven just isn't a good debut work and she admitted that. It's got a slow start, a unique concept (if I do say so myself), and I don't have enough credentials to make a reputable agent take a chance on me.

So I set it aside. I finished writing the sequel to Haven, Avalon, that I'd stopped working on when I decided to get serious about my editing. My finances were more stable now, so I reached out to an editor I'd become friends with on twitter and she agreed to do a developmental edit for me at a significant discount.

While we were discussing all the changes that I needed to make to Avalon, she mentioned that I should start thinking about self publishing. Few agents were willing to take on a debut like mine and even fewer were willing to take on a fully written series. It was very likely that the only way I'd be able to see Avalon published along with Haven was if I put them out myself.

I wrestled with it. Traditional publishing is a fiercely competitive industry. Agents routinely get 100+ queries in a single day and few publishing houses are willing to take on unagented writers. Getting an agent and then finding a publisher would take at least another year. From there, it'd be two-three more years before my book would actually hit the shelves. The wheels of publishing move slowly and I wanted to get Haven out in the world.

So I hired my editor friend again to proof-read Haven, trimmed three thousand more words, and reached out to my self-published friend to make a plan. I got a cover made, bought ISBNs, and got my pre-orders prepared.

I nearly cried when I held my proof for the first time. In my hands was the culmination of five years' work and a lifetime of dreaming.

And it never would've happened if Dad hadn't decided to watch Indiana Jones that day.

15

The Bad: I've Never Been Good With Directions

There are things that everyone knows. Things that people take for granted because they've always been there and will continue to be there. Things like the movement of the sun, the effects of gravity, and MacLeods standing up during high-stakes board games.

Things like me having absolutely no sense of direction.

Seriously, I joke to this day that I'd get lost if I got stuck in a round room with one clearly lit exit. I used a GPS to get to my office every day for the first six months I worked at my first job. I can't consistently find my way to a townhouse my parents' own despite the fact that someone I'm related to has lived there for almost ten years.

Directions go in one ear and out the other and 90% of the reason I wanted a smartphone was having constant access to a GPS.

It's a part of myself that I've long since accepted and I've taken measures to minimize the impact my lack of internal compass has on others.

Unfortunately, it took a long time for me to accept that and this story was a big part of that journey.

For as long as I can remember, my family travelled to Minneapolis each year. My Dad had a medical conference of some sort in town and that was probably important, but to us kids there was only one thing that mattered in the entire city:

The Mall of America and the Camp Snoopy theme park.

Now, I know I'm aging myself a little here, but even before Nickelodeon bought out the theme park, it was one of my favorite places to be. Camp Snoopy was the largest indoor amusement park in the country at the time and it was hopping. There were rollercoasters, water rides, a haunted mansion, and a kite-eating tree ride I honestly love to this day.

There was also a merry-go-round and for a four-year-old who was obsessed with princesses and fairy tales, it was the best thing in the world. It had horses, carriages, tigers, and enough light bulbs to blind a bat.

It was beautiful.

Unfortunately, my brothers and sisters didn't really want to spend all day riding the merry-go-round when there were rollercoasters, water rides, and a haunted mansion. They wanted to ride the fun, big-kid rides my sisters and I weren't tall enough to go on or were outright terrified of. Since my parents wisely decreed that one of the big kids had to be with the little kids at all times and that the big kids were in charge, I didn't get to ride the merry-go-round nearly often enough to make the five hour drive worth it. After all, we only had a day at the amusement park and we needed to take advantage of each available Moment we had before the rides shut down and we wouldn't see them for another year.

The second best thing about this annual trip was getting to eat at "fancy" restaurants. The Rainforest Cafe might not seem like much, but even on a doctor's budget, ten people's a crowd and it had enough moving parts to entertain even the most distracted four-year-old. And, to make things even better, Mom promised me that we could ride the merry-go-round one more time when we were done.

The Rainforest Cafe was all the way on the other side of the mall from Camp Snoopy—probably less than a quarter mile to be honest—and my little legs felt each agonizingly slow step. And since my older sisters wanted to do some window shopping as we went, it felt even longer.

Luckily, to my little eyes, I could see the park from here. The indoor ferris wheel was massive and I could definitely find my way to the merry-go-round from there. The others clearly didn't understand the importance of the merry-go-round, otherwise they wouldn't be taking so long.

That or they didn't know where it was and they didn't want to admit it. While I was ruminating over my situation and admittedly getting angry that I was going to lose my chance to ride the merry-go-round, a solution presented itself in my mind with all the aplomb of an Einstein Moment.

I was a little kid and the big kids (and Mom) were supposed to look after me. If I ran ahead, they'd have to follow me and I could take them straight to the merry-go-round! Maybe we'd even have time to ride it twice!

Seeing no problems with this plan, I waited until Mom looked away for a Moment and took off down the escalators.

At first, the plan went beautifully. I ran straight to the merry-go-round and spun around to point it out to the others—except they weren't there.

No matter, I told myself, casting a longing glance at the bright lights of the merry-go-round, I'll just backtrack a little. They can't be far behind.

It was right about then that the holes in my brilliant plan presented itself.

The Mall of America is big. Really big. Way bigger than my four-year-old self realized. It has three floors, many wings, and countless shops that all look the same when you can't read. And it has many, many escalators.

I took an escalator upstairs again and didn't see my family. By this time I was getting a little scared and decided to find my way back to the merry-go-round to wait. I reasoned that Mom knew that's where I wanted to go so she'd surely go straight there.

Except what little me didn't realize was that she'd likely come and gone in the time between me backtracking and me realizing I didn't know where I'd left them.

So I went back to the merry-go-round and I waited. And no one I knew came to find me.

So I did the only logical thing I could. I started crying.

As my siblings will attest, I'm a very loud individual. My parents used to use me as a secondary alarm clock when my brothers didn't want to get out of bed.

As it turns out, a four-year-old sobbing and screaming for her Mom draws a lot of attention. A security officer found me and brought me back to their offices. I can't say it was easy for him because my Dad has always been a big proponent of a violent reaction to strange men trying to grab you, but he got me there.

His next big problem was trying to figure out who I was. I knew my own name, but hadn't quite grasped that my parents might be called something other than Mom and Dad. What's worse, I couldn't even describe my Mom properly because she'd chosen to wear a skirt that day and I didn't know that word. The officers had to find Mom based on my name and the description of "a blonde woman in a half-dress and shirt".

Luckily, MacLeod isn't a common name in the Midwest and there was only one MacLeod family visiting the Mall of America that day that had lost a red-headed little girl prone to screaming fits when she was upset.

Mom found me eventually and was too relieved to have me back to immediately give me the lecture I undoubtedly deserved. Once I had her in sight, my anxiety virtually disappeared and I busied myself with the goody bag the nice security officers had given me to make me stop screaming.

I eventually got that lecture and probably a few more from siblings who were very upset I had to hold their hand now, but that goody bag had CDs, posters, and candy, so little me would probably say it was worth it.

Of course, I'll still admit a touch of bitterness to finding out Mom gave those CDs to my older sisters, rightly determining that I shouldn't have gotten a reward for running off and that I had no interest in the Backstreet boys.

I can't say that was the last time I've run off over the years, but I've gotten loads better at finding myself and where I am relative to the people I came with. Having a phone helps, but knowing all those lovely descriptive words like skirt, glasses, and blouse certainly helps.

16

The Ugly: Why Armchairs Make Me Nervous

I was a profoundly clumsy child who turned into a clumsy teenager and then a clumsy adult. My elementary school principal used to joke that he was afraid to take his eyes off me because I might hurt myself again.

To be fair, it wasn't an unfair assessment. My body is a map of small scars from a lifetime of not looking where I was going. I've broken both my wrists, ruptured a tendon in my pinky, gotten stitches three times, needed surgery to repair a torn meniscus, and sprained my ankles and wrists more times than I like to think about.

Out of all of these, the injury that stands out most happened when I was six and playing hide and seek with my twin sister, Chris.

I didn't particularly want to play, but our Mom insisted. She didn't, however, say I had to put any real effort into it. Which is why I chose to hide behind an armchair in the living room instead of somewhere Chris might miss me.

My parents had recently remodelled the living room and put in a beautiful bay window looking out into the front yard. This particular armchair sat in the living room through this entire process and they used it as a place to hold their tools.

Unbeknownst to them, a box cutter fell into the cracks in the armchair (although Brett has apparently confessed to dropping it down there) and got thoroughly stuck in the leg rest mechanisms. At the time of this incident, its blade stuck out the back of the armchair like a particularly big thorn.

If you think little me would be cautious about that, you should be aware that I'd never seen a rosebush and didn't understand the dangers of thorns.

So I didn't see any harm in kicking the back of the armchair while I waited for Chris to find me.

And then I slipped. My foot hit the back of the armchair and it spun. The box cutter dug into my arm like a knife through hot butter.

I don't actually think the cut itself hurt that much, but the scar is nearly two inches long and a quarter-inch wide as an adult so it must have hurt a lot. My oldest sister, who admits she's squeamish and might be exaggerating a bit, said she could see bone.

Either way, it was certainly something to see on my tiny arm.

That alone would be a horrifying event, but it gets much worse.

I didn't want to get in trouble for hurting myself like that—even then I realized I probably shouldn't have been playing behind that armchair to begin with—so I decided the best thing to do was handle it myself.

At the time, I was reading through the Wheel of Time and my favorite character was the healer, Nynaeve. I knew from her that injuries needed to be cleaned before they were bandaged. It was unclear how, exactly, they were meant to be cleaned, but since she was a well-known healer and also an adult she clearly knew what she was doing.

By my six-year-old logic, that meant I should tramp across the house to my parents bathroom (far superior to the bathroom five feet from where I'd injured myself, which was scary and also stunk since my brothers used it) and wash it in their sink.

Leaving a trail of blood behind me, I raced down the hall to my parents room, stuck my arm under their faucet, and turned it on full blast.

My memory cuts out there. Honestly, it's probably why I don't remember the initial injury hurting much because that hurt a lot. By comparison, a little (big) cut wasn't much to write home about at all.

I've asked various family members what happened next and from what I've gathered I screamed. Loudly.

Jen says she freaked out when she saw what I'd done.

Katie says she grabbed a washcloth and wrapped it around my arm to stem the bleeding.

Chris went to get Mom.

I'm almost certain none of my brothers were there, but I honestly couldn't say for sure.

I don't think I'll ever get an entirely straight answer about what happened. I soaked through three washcloths by the time we got to the emergency room and that was after I'd trailed blood across the house, so the bathroom must've looked like a murder scene. For the more squeamish members of my family, it must've been a nightmare.

The first thing I remember after sticking my arm under the faucet is being angry that I had to wear my little sister's pink crocs to the emergency room. They were uncomfortable, small, and worst of all, pink.

It might seem like a strange thing to be upset about, but when you're the sixth of eight kids, and a twin, you get really particular about what's yours and what's not. Also I think my blood was mostly adrenaline at that point so my mental facilities weren't all there.

Mom seemed to think that dealing with the bleeding gash on my arm was more important than finding my shoes, so off we went to the ER. Any other day and I'd have been thrilled that I got to sit in the front seat, but by then the shock was wearing off and I knew I'd seriously messed up. Little me was very apologetic about ruining three of Mom's dish towels by bleeding through them, but she assured me it was fine.

When we got to the hospital, I was rushed into the back and laid on a big white table in a bright and scary room. I don't remember much from here either. Between shock, fear, and pain, I was worn out and exhausted so I didn't struggle while they worked.

It took ten stitches to close up the cut. At school the next day, I'd be the coolest person in the classroom since I had a bandage that covered half my arm, but at that time I just wanted to go home and cuddle with Mom.

If I squint, I can still make out the scars the thread left behind. The main scar has faded some, but an untimely sunburn covered half of it in a freckle that has had more than one person asking me if it's skin cancer.

It's a useful marker, both because it's a fun story and because it gives me a decent margin for pain any other time I've seriously injured myself.

Of course, this can backfire dramatically. In the years since, it took half a day to realize I'd hurt myself the first time I broke my wrist, two days and a basketball game the second time I broke my wrist, and six months for me to realize I'd done something more than pulled my hamstring when I tore the meniscus in my knee.

I've slowed down on the injury front in recent years, but it's too much to hope that's because I've learned something from my clumsiness over the years. More likely, it's because I've slowed down and I don't deal as much damage when I hit something at a walk than at a dead sprint.

Still, I'm looking forward to the future. May it bring me many more years of interesting injuries and funny looking scars.

On a completely unrelated note, I'm putting Mom up for sainthood for getting me to adulthood when I was bound and determined to run off and injure myself at the slightest provocation. Dad gets it for putting me back together each time I break myself.

17

Chris

The Good: Libérer le Bébé!

My memories start fairly early, and there are very few in which my younger sister, Bridget, is not featured prominently.

I remember in the months before she arrived, a lot of promises were made. Erin and I received the announcement "special" (one on one with Mom and Dad) since we were the youngest, and were losing our positions as "the baby" (a title we fought for—we'd alternate days on which we'd get to be the youngest). We had a lot of questions about what this meant—mainly concerning where this new baby was going to sleep, as Erin and I were in "the nursery", the room right by Mom and Dad's room. We argued it wasn't fair to have to move, since the basement where the rest of the kids slept was prime monster territory (a monster lived in the laundry room and we had one in the costume closet—our home was considered prime real estate to the entrepreneurial monster). Reassurances were made by Dad that if we did have to move, he would perform monster checks every night. He also said it would be our choice if we moved, but if we didn't move we'd need to share our room with the baby, which probably wouldn't be fun.

We would ask our Mom if the baby was here yet just about every day. Erin and I would trade off who got to ask Mom if the baby was here, although at some point my mother shared with us that Dad worked at the hospital, and the baby was coming from there so it might be worth asking him.

We'd wait until Dad was home from work and run up to him, trying to see if he had the new baby. He'd reassure us we would definitely know when the baby arrived, and they put the date on the calendar (a strange device on that wall that tracked the days of the week). We had a countdown for when the new baby was coming—and everything about it was a surprise. We didn't know the name, or if it was a boy or a girl.

The day arrived.

The reader should stop at this Moment to acknowledge I was two-and-a-half at this point. My experience with babies extended to my twin sister, who could do everything I could do.

The baby was extremely disappointing.

To the great disappointment of my youngest-older brother (how we differentiated—there was oldest-older brother, Ryan, and youngest-older brother, Brett, and middle-older brother, Scott), the baby was a girl. I remember him venting that it was unfair he didn't have a younger brother since Ryan and Scott both got the experience and he just got to have younger sisters. Erin thought we were being unfair to Mom and Dad for having a girl, but I remember agreeing with Brett because I already had a young sister—Erin! They really could have planned better.

Bridget couldn't do anything. My older siblings promised that younger siblings were great—it was a new friend you were related to! They forgot to mention it takes forever for the baby to learn how to play. She couldn't eat, and we tried testing lots of foods. Dad was very vehement only Mom or he could feed the baby but Erin and I agreed they were bad at it since Bridget was so slow at learning how to eat. I have a vivid memory of us waving bread in front of her face when they weren't looking. This resulted in us having limited unsupervised time with Bridget. The nice thing about being twins is you have a built-in distraction—we would team up and one would decide to "get in trouble" while the other "played" with Bridget. As many, many, many people in the family will share, potatoes were the "soul saver". They were her favorite food but they were boring.

Erin and I agreed that Bridget's first Christmas was extremely disappointing. As far as "first presents" went, I don't remember what she received, but I think that really validates my feelings about the entire holiday. By this time Bridget could sit up and was much better at playing. We weren't allowed any candy, no matter how much we asked or told our parents Bridget really needed candy. She really didn't have a handle on the sneakiness that Erin and I had mastered.

You will notice in most of this story it's a lot of "Erin and I" as we did everything together—we were the same age, slept in the same bed, and spent a majority of our days together. Eventually, this evolved into "the twins and Bridget" and finally, "the girls".

My next largest memory was being told Bridget couldn't have playtime. She had to nap all the time. We thought it was unfair, and tried to devise different ways to get her out. Keep in mind, as an adult my memory construes this as vehement planning conversations with diagrams involved. I'm sure I was a lot less verbose and imaginative than my pride allows me to remember.

Bridget and Mom had similar nap times. At the start of the day, you'd ask an "adult" (anyone over the age of seven) if you had to nap today, and if Bridget needed an extra nap. Generally, we had a morning nap, and an afternoon nap, and Bridget had a lunch nap or a dinner nap. The next step of the plan was to get an older and wiser sibling. As they aged, they were less likely to help us liberate the baby, even though I have memories of being coached out of my own crib with Erin by some of the siblings who refused, although I won't point fingers.

Jen and Katie were out—both were too responsible, we agreed. The next steps were Ryan, Scott, and Brett. Ryan and Scott were a tag team, and you had to catch them in a mischievous mood when they weren't grounded. Finally, there was Brett, who was a solid pick, except he often didn't want to play with toddlers, instead, he wanted to play with his brothers. If Ryan and Scott weren't playing, he didn't want to be involved. This meant you had to be devious and separate the trio. Brett—if you are reading this remember I was three, but I do apologize for causing you emotional distress. I'll add I truly thought it was for the greater good and that Bridget was in baby jail and unfairly grounded.

To separate the trio, you needed Brett to throw a tantrum, so that Ryan and Scott would be fed up with him for being little. You wanted to start fights between the three of them, and that way you had a higher shot of one giving in. You didn't want them to realize the plan, because of course that would mean they definitely wouldn't help free Bridget. This could be accomplished through small annoyances, like stealing shoes, "accidentally" spilling something on the target right as they were about to run outside and play, or pretending to be hurt so they had to take care of you, and wasn't it a coincidence? The only thing that could possibly cheer you up was going to see the baby.

Luckily, Brett forgave Bridget for being a girl, as he became enamored with the baby as well. We liked to brag about how far along she was learning, and prod her to speak (she only knew about five words at the time). Brett was a genius, he already could tie his shoes and he was learning to write. He could do no wrong if he was on our side.

Brett was the one who pointed out which floorboards were squeaky, and figured out how to tell the time in half-hour increments (he figured out what the larger hand meant but not what the numbers meant). When my parents replaced the clock with a digital clock, we were lucky all of us already knew how to tell time. Brett had a good idea on hiding places and had a much longer reach, meaning he could carry the baby. He was about five though and a one-year-old is pretty heavy at that age so he usually set her down as soon as we escaped the room.

After our morning nap, Mom might have fallen asleep next to Bridget's crib. If you knew which floorboards to avoid, you could sneak right up to the crib and see the baby. It was important to know the mood Bridget would be in, and we'd tell her to be quiet if she wanted to play. Sometimes Bridget would be annoyed we'd woken her up and she'd start crying, at which point you had to hide. Favorite places included under the bed, in the closets, and if you were desperate, behind the door. Brett was usually fast enough he could escape out the door, and keep an eye out for older kids coming to check on the baby as well.

I'm not sure if my Mom knew we were hiding and accepted it as a part of having children or if she was extremely sleep deprived from having eight children.

You'd wait until Mom had calmed Bridget down (usually picking her up from the crib, which was unfair seeing as you didn't get carried anywhere anymore since you were so big) and wait until both fell asleep. Then you'd climb up to the crib and wave at the baby again—and repeat.

Getting caught meant a lecture from Mom and a time out. Getting caught a second time was a longer time out. Getting caught a third time was a lecture from Dad. We tried to recruit the older siblings into the libérer le bébé front, but most refused oddly enough.

Eventually, when Bridget learned to stand and understood what we were doing, she'd reach her arms up and we had a reasonable defense to say "But DAD, she wanted out of the crib!". The Dad Justice System was clearly biased against young children, and we didn't have lawyers present, resulting in unconstitutional groundings. He would give you time to state your case, and then render his decision, generally, a fifteen-minute time out, which was enough time for you to cool down from the emotional impact of unjustly getting into trouble.

Getting Bridget out of the crib (if Brett wasn't there) involved one twin standing on the other, grabbing Bridget by the hands, and pulling as hard as you could. It usually resulted in a dog pile of toddlers. Key instincts involve protecting the baby's head, otherwise she will cry and wake Mom. To this day I actually think cribs are meant to protect against interfering siblings, and are not for the baby's protection. We used to have a wooden crib, but the parents got rid of it when they discovered walking babies couldn't stay in it. They'd pretend to put us to sleep, and then watch through the crack in the door to see if we escaped. There were several loose pegs you could knock out if you had the dexterity, and after several tries with screws and wood glue my father gave in and decided they either needed a new crib, or they could use the pack 'n' play, which had the advantage of being several feet closer to the ground for interfering toddlers.

Once you have liberated the baby, send a twin to ask a sibling for the time, and ask for the time when Bridget usually wakes up (the key is to lie and look innocent, like you truly believe the baby is still asleep in her crib). You ask how long that is, and ask if they can get you ten minutes beforehand so you are ready to play with her. The sibling in question may be suspicious, but they don't have enough "adult" in them to question why you are asking this. You had to pick siblings carefully—those over thirteen had too much adult in them and would question why you wanted to know, or worse, teach you to tell time. Those under seven couldn't tell time. When Brett learned to tell time the libérer le bébé front celebrated, as it meant unlimited playtime. He would either play with us and the baby or come through and remind us to put her back in her crib.

Getting the baby back in the crib is much harder than liberating the baby. You now have a non-sneaky baby who doesn't know the squeaky floors, and you will need to unceremoniously chuck the baby into the crib, which may result in crying. You may or may not spend about ten minutes having the baby practice falling so they don't cry. You may have your older brother practice weight lifting the baby so he can make it over the crib wall. I do remember sneaking Bridget cheese and bread to stay quiet while we snuck her back in, as long as she finished her snack before Mom woke up. My Mom was a bit confused on days where Bridget "woke" from her nap messier than when she'd been put down.

If Mom wakes up early, you resume your hiding place, you wait until she leaves the room with the baby, and then you run around the opposite stairs she went down (there were two sets). This gave you an alibi that you were on the other side of the house. Bonus points if a twin was randomly found in that part of the house during "naptime".

The plan didn't always work, and my memories could absolutely be faulty. I'm sure we failed to liberate her more times than we succeeded, and to be completely honest, we'd only get about ten or twenty minutes of playtime out of it, and afterwards be completely exhausted and voluntarily take a nap (a capital crime to a toddler). If Mom or Dad ask if the baby left her crib at all, because she is rather grouchy, now is a good time to remind them you are a toddler and don't have a good memory. You've lost "the game" if Mom and Dad unfairly ground you even though they have no proof because Bridget can't even speak and as twins you never give in—snitches get stitches.

It is one of my fondest memories though.

Libérer le bébé!

18

The Bad: Vedo un Piccione!

When I was in third grade, my parents decided we needed to see the world to become more educated. My aunt and uncle had recently returned from Rome, and had wonderful stories on the religious awakening a pilgrimage could have. Their kids were finally old enough to travel, they had no need for a diaper bag, and most of us were more well-behaved. At this point, Jen and Katie were in college, and were unable to join us. I'll stop for a moment to acknowledge that this was an amazing opportunity, and I am grateful for my parents for providing it to us.

Pre-trip, we were told to do preparation. We needed to prove we could pack quickly, and were instructed we'd need our passports on us at all times. We had been on plenty of planes before, but we were warned this one would be the longest yet—eight hours in flight. My Mom looked up tips for what we could do, and reminded us it would be more like a car trip, you could get up to go to the bathroom when you needed to but that was it, you weren't allowed to really stretch your legs. She tried to be conscientious and didn't want a stranger stuck with two fighting eight-year-olds. She had larger children (my father is a little over 6'7"), so she tried to pick exit rows for her husband and sons, and she volunteered to sit with the girls.

The trip there was uneventful (for the most part). I remember being stuck in O'Hare airport for several hours in their international terminal where there was nothing to do (my Gameboy had died). The memory is so traumatic I have flashbacks whenever I land there, and warned my husband when he was picking flights that I didn't want to stop in Chicago. I apologize to the people of Chicago, but the city planner really should have thought that out before they offended an eight-year-old with boring architecture and no playground in the international wing of the airport.

We landed in Paris, and I'm still a bit bitter at my father for this next part. The time they had chosen to schedule this trip fell right during the Presidential Fitness Exam—which meant all of us got out of doing the mile run at school. For those unaware, the PFE is a standard list of times and repetitions all children of a certain age should be able to complete—those unable to meet the requirements are at risk of being in poor health. This meant doing so many jumping jacks, pushups, proving your flexibility, and completing the Mile Run, which as the reader can guess is how fast you can run a mile. Most MacLeod kids disliked the mile run to my memory, because, at heart, we were "sit down and read/play video games" children. We were in sports out of an obligation to fitness, at least until we got to high school.

The fact our pilgrimage was scheduled over the PFE meant an escape from the mile run and the long-dreaded exercise. We were ecstatic.

Looking back, I should have known what would happen, as this is my father.

Our flight from the airport landed on one end of the Parisian airport, and of course, our flight that needed to board in the next half hour was on the other end, six miles away. What followed is entitled in family history as "The Sprint through the Paris Airport". Now, my memory has definitely exaggerated this, and I wasn't exactly focused on capturing the memory honestly, I was focusing on my breath and rather mad I was having to time myself running, the exact thing I'd been gleeful at avoiding.

We sprinted down escalators, Bridget at one point was scooped up and carried fireman style through some tram doors. I'm sure details are embellished, but I have a vivid memory of Ryan jumping at least two sets of stairs. Imagine for a Moment, ten large Americans, with limited luggage (my parents are vehemently against checking luggage—and as an adult, so am I. It's a scam), charging through your airport. My father was physically blind in one eye, so those on his right tended to meet their end when he took particularly wide left turns. We arrived at the gate just as the doors closed. There were a few tense moments. The security guard reminded my father that sprinting through an airport can cause a panic, so in the future would he mind not doing so and just calling ahead?

We boarded the bus that took us to the plane that would take us to Italy.

I slept the whole way, and the Italian couple next to me gave me a soda and sandwich, as they thought I was traveling alone and they didn't want me to miss lunch. I would later have a dream of that same Italian couple adopting me, and not having to run anywhere again.

I think the Paris airport gave my Dad PTSD in traveling. He has since insisted on being at least one day early, or scheduling five hours between his flights to ensure he won't be late. Upon landing all the children begged our parents to email the school and let them know we had passed the PFE with stellar times, worried we had run six miles already and upon arriving back in America we'd need to run another. "I will faint if I have to run one more step," a brother proudly declared before passing out between jet lag and physical exhaustion.

The joke was once again on us. Anyone who has used the Italian bussing system understands you will walk at least fifteen miles a day.

The pilgrimage was incredibly enjoyable—we tried foods we had never heard of before, we tried (and failed) to learn Italian from our tour guide, Luca. About halfway through the trip though, it took a dramatic left turn into chaos. The reader should understand our family is divided on the incident in Venice. One side claims that Bridget and I ran off into the middle of the Venetian square, never to be seen again. Bridget and I, though, are in agreement, and here is my opportunity to share the real story of what happened in Venice.

The day before the incident, we were briefed on the history of Venice, and how different it was from every other city. Erin and I had prepared by primarily reading fiction that featured Italian cities, and our favorite at the time was The Thief, a story by Cornelia Funk about two orphans who run away to Venice and are adopted into a gang of street children. Cornelia Funk described Venice as a city of wonder and magic. When we arrived, we'd point out different parts of the architecture mentioned in the story, and we wondered where Scipio's theatre would be. We were most impressed with the number of pigeons in the city. We don't really have pigeons in North Dakota, and these were considered an exotic animal to us. We thought they were gorgeous and would name our favorite ones. City dwellers would laugh at this, and our parents tried to explain that pigeons were considered pests, but we wouldn't hear of it.

I stand by this opinion as an adult. Pigeons are majestic creatures and are doves that need to deal with colorism.

Venice had a lot of pigeons, and we were enamored. My parents wouldn't allow us to feed the pigeons, but they let us watch the salespeople who had pigeon feed, and allowed us to pet them. Pigeons are a part of church life—they roost in the bell towers and on the statues, and are accepted as such. Our tour guide mentioned it was considered lucky if a church had a family of pigeons, and my favorite pope was chosen because a "dove" (a pigeon in disguise), landed on his head in St. Peter's square while the cardinals debated on who the next Pope should be. Luca knew how to share his country's culture and make the whole experience magical. While he himself wasn't religious, our tour specified we attend daily mass, and so each day we visited a new church—never attending mass in the same place twice. Erin and I talked about how lucky Italians were, that they could sit in these century-old churches and they had their pick, having multiple churches within walking distance!

You reached Venice by ferry, and the ride over was delightful. Nothing describes the feeling when the city comes into view. I've returned since then, and the feeling is the same. Venice is a gorgeous city flooded (quite literally) with Italian culture and history, and it would be a shame for the city to be lost. It's one of the reasons I became concerned about global warming as a young child. I wanted my own children to have the experience for themselves.

Back to the pigeons.

During our midday break, the three girls were running around the square, trying to pet pigeons. We'd been given a rule to stay within ten feet of our parents, which I will adamantly defend we were doing. Bridget and I were holding hands, and when we turned around, our entire family was gone.

You are eight, you have your five-year-old sister with you, and you don't speak Italian. In that moment we were Bo and Prospero—lost in Venice. This Moment probably lasted about ten minutes, but to my memory I approximately aged ten years. We decided to wait five minutes, and if five minutes had passed and our family hadn't returned for us, we would find a police officer and show them the tag that said in Italian "Hello, I am _____, I am with Glory Tours, and I am lost. Please contact them at.....". The problem, we discovered, is Italian police officers don't wear the same uniforms as American police officers. We most likely passed one or two, but didn't recognize them for what they were.

We stayed in the square.

Another five minutes passed. I would swear to you, the clouds darkened, and I thought about when I last ate, and became concerned it was my last meal. I decided to find the ferry we'd come in on. We'd been told to meet up at the ferry at the end of the day, and I figured we'd be safer at the ferry, waiting several hours and "wasting" the day than wandering around the city.

We held hands and walked back to the ferry, the problem being we'd been so focused on looking at Venice when we arrived we never really memorized what our boat looked like. We stood on a bridge, overlooking the docks, and became extremely overwhelmed. Bridget and I had a conversation about the next plan, and she asked to go back to the square we'd started in. I agreed, and we wandered back.

The docks are one block away from the square, if that. It was two turns. Upon entering the square, a strong arm grabbed my shoulder and I almost screamed. It was my brother, who looked relieved. He waved down my Dad, who lectured us on running away, refusing to listen to the fact we'd been abandoned. Unjustly, we were "grounded" for the rest of the trip and each of the girls was assigned a brother to hold hands with for the rest of the trip, something Erin was extremely ticked off about since she hadn't run away. Bridget and I were mad since we were adamant we hadn't run away, and our brothers were mad that they were assigned babysitting for the rest of the trip. My parents were upset because they believed they'd almost lost two daughters.

Suffice to say, no one was happy.

The rest of the trip was amazing, and relatively uneventful, but we were lectured severely for telling anyone we were abandoned, and that we had run away, even having to correct our reports on Italy to our teacher (she'd amended our lesson plan and provided our lessons ahead of time). My family doesn't understand, we were Bo and Prospero, looking for our Aunt in Venice.

This story doesn't compare to the time my father abandoned Bridget in Egypt, but I will let her tell that story.

19

The Ugly: Gute Gewohnheiten zum Leben

The following is ugly in that it involves multiple injuries to children, and quite a few stories my parents don't know, or don't remember. There are mentions of blood, broken bones, drowning, fire, child labour, and the breaking of multiple pinky promises. May my family's trauma bring you a few smiles.

My parents didn't really have formal rules—as we aged they came and went and different children had different rules, which was simultaneously unfair and wise. The rules we had as children varied widely between us—for a long time they had a rule that stated "no singing at the table" for my twin sister, Erin. They also went through a phase where anytime you did something mean to a sibling, you had to find something to compliment them on. That rule quickly faded when my brother Ryan found he could speed his way through trouble by saying "I like your shoes, I like your hair, I like your smile," and move on, because Ryan was all about loopholes.

Still, there were consistent themes I recall being taught.

Rule 1: Listen to parents

This rule is fairly straightforward—parents were considered any adults with children. My parents wanted us to recognize authority figures and show us there were people we could learn from, and that children may not always be the best examples.

There are many examples I can think of for when I decided this rule made sense (because as a child you instantly want to figure out how to break any rule you are taught). The earliest time I can remember thinking "maybe these people know a little more than I" I was a toddler, and it was bath time. My Mom instructed me NOT to touch or go near the razor that my father had left on the counter. This clearly was an incentive to gun for it when her back was turned. I had seen my Dad shave his face, so I was curious what would happen if I dragged it across my stomach, because I'm a scientist at heart.

When my Mom turned back around, there was a lot of blood, and Bridget saw I had the razor, and decided she too should give it a try.

As it turned out we had very minor cuts, and my toddler brain was just thoroughly traumatized from the incident. So much so, that it impacted my impression of men, and how brave they must be to shave every single day, when razors were the things of nightmares.

After that incident, I decided my mother must be somewhat wise, as she had tried to prevent me from learning that.

The lesson did not stick—my mother still complains about the Holocaust project that is responsible for three separate kitchen fires. The project consisted of creating a box a Holocaust survivor might have put together, based on stories and biographies we read throughout the year. Part of this project was to make the box and artifacts look old.

With the first child (I don't remember who), my Mom suggested slightly burning the paper letters they'd written over our gas stove. This was done in a supervised manner, and still resulted in the letters in flames in the kitchen sink.

Having learned her lesson, my Mom cautioned against the method with the next child to do the project (Brett). Brett decided to forego flame, and instead dipped his letters in lemon juice and placed them in the oven. I do not know if this was supervised, but I do know the letters and a dish towel were lost to the cause in the crusade to make authentic fake Holocaust relics.

When my turn to complete this project came around, my mother told me the stories of my siblings, and advised not to use any heat at all, and recommended tea bags, soaking the letters in muddy water, and using lemon juice if necessary.

I waited until my Mom left to run errands and immediately tried burning my letters, because I thought it would add "authentic flair" and I was clearly wiser than my siblings.

My Mom returned to a smoky kitchen and a very guilty seventh child. I knew I'd been caught, but rather than a lecture, my Mom simply emailed my teacher, having given up on any of her children learning, and asked her to let other parents know flames should not be used to "age" letters, and could she please remove the part of the project that gave points on appearances for being "burned," since she was planning on re-doing her floors soon.

I learned that day that my Mom might know a thing or two about raising children, and she might be worth listening to, but she knew there are some things you just don't learn until you try it yourself.

Rule 2: Don't go on the roof

This was my favorite rule as a child simply because it seemed impossible to achieve. It was created after a very spirited evening of "night games" (cops and robbers, freeze tag, etc.). After chasing several kids off his roof, my Dad let everyone know he was updating the rules, and now out of bounds was considered the property line, inside the house, and on top of the roof. He then launched into a lecture on why running on a roof at night in fall might be dangerous, but I don't remember the finer points.

The point is, he had just issued a challenge and didn't know it. A new game was created that night: how often can you get on the roof and not get in trouble?

Ryan took this challenge to heart, and even at one point faked a head injury with red dye and corn syrup to play a prank. As children, Erin and I weren't interested in breaking the rule, but we were entertained by following the boys around the house, and subsequently laughing when my Dad pulled into the driveway to see several of his kids on the roof.

A secondary rule was added: if you see a child on the roof and don't tell an adult, you will be grounded.

Rule 3: No swimming without an adult

There is an injustice in being small and not knowing how to do things. There is a competitive side in all of us, that strives to compete and learn when we see another human do a task we have not figured out.

Swimming lessons were required for us growing up. My parents liked to camp, and visit lakes and the ocean. It was a given we'd be swimming at all times, and they took careful precautions for their children who hadn't mastered it. They always had life jackets and floaties available, with plenty on hand for guests. Swimming as an activity was designated the lowest bar; that is, if you had two children and one knew how to swim and one couldn't, you were not allowed in rough water or water that went above your chest. You had to play in the area that all of you could play or you couldn't swim at all.

We had a pool growing up, and my parents recognized it wouldn't be fair to limit their teenagers to what their youngest children could do. Older children could reserve the pool with advance notice and swim without worrying about younger children. My parents had baby gates and a system specifically in place to prevent the following story, because my father's nightmare was one of us was going to drown when he least expected.

We did like to compare "have you ever drowned" stories when he wasn't around.

My story was pretty good, because I accomplished breaking several rules. I was in the pool room without an adult, during a reserved "older kids" time, and I decided I didn't want to wear my life jacket or floaties.

I convinced Erin to go swimming with me, and told the big kids Mom had said we could (we were at an age where it was slightly plausible). Erin and I began challenging each other to go deeper into the pool, which was about seven feet deep at its worst, and three feet in the shallow end. Finally, in a bid to be declared winner, I announced I had just learned to swim and very proudly walked straight off into the deep end of the pool.

Fact check: I had not learned to swim.

I quickly realized I made a poor decision, and discovered that while Ariel makes it look easy, breathing underwater is actually surprisingly difficult. I began flailing my limbs to no avail, and my vision began going dark.

The next thing I knew, I was being dragged up by an arm, and I was launched over the side of the pool, where I promptly threw up a lot of chlorinated water, and my oatmeal breakfast.

Scott had noticed me drowning, and had put his Boy Scout skills to use.

"Chris," he said, "stay out of the deep end. It's for big kids. And don't tell Dad." He then nodded sagely and swam off.

I asked Erin if we could go play barbies and slept for a few hours.

I never went swimming without telling an adult again.

Rule 4: No biking without an adult

The injustice in not knowing how to do things continues. Just about every kid has the story of when they learned to ride a bike. Their parents may have gotten them a practice bike, which is just a bike you walk with and use your feet to brake.

The prime part of this is your parents probably didn't buy you a bike until you learned how to ride one. The issue here is you can't learn without one. There are those who propose what seems to be a simple solution, which is to borrow a sibling's bike. To those I say, you clearly have never had siblings.

Having many siblings, shared spaces, and a life of "hand-me-down" days, you grow protective of the things that are yours. Learning to share is an experience that is filled with highs and lows, and I will be the first to admit even as an adult I struggle with sharing.

Part of this story is inspired from a conversation between my two nephews, one who was ten at the time, and one who was two. The two-year-old is just learning to share, now that his younger sister is more mobile and vocal about interacting with the world. He was horrified to discover that instead of her simply playing with the toys he handed her, she would have preferences. Much consolation has come from my sister-in-law, who explained the concept of sharing, and that toys can be used by multiple people, while still remaining "yours", on the other hand, some toys are everybody's.

My ten-year-old nephew is relatively ok with the concept of sharing, as far as ten-year-olds go. He was a bit shocked the concept had to be learned versus being innate. Their interactions as the older one slowly learned that some toys were not ok to play with because the toddler wasn't ok with sharing them yet reminded me of times when I was a two-year-old, and being frustrated that everything was Erin's and mine, never just mine.

Couple this with the competitive twin streak, and what you have is a race for who can bike before the other. It is a challenge, and because of Mom's "no biking/unicycling/rollerblading in the house" you are restricted to practicing during the summertime when your siblings aren't using their bikes. I have distinct memories of walking through the 788 house, and measuring the height of a bike next to me (we were only allowed to alter the bike's height if we changed it back when we were done, and that took more strength than we had, plus you had to find someone to do it for you). If you were desperate, you just accepted you weren't going to sit while you learned.

After finding your bike, you find a large hill, jump on, and hope you don't fall.

I remember those instructions distinctly, as my brothers were directed to teach us, and they had a belief that "less is more" when it came to instruction. You will note the use of helmets is not included, until my father caught us pushing each other into the ditch (a six-foot incline), in the hopes we'd garner enough speed to keep our balance, helmet-less, on Ryan's and Scott's bikes. I think Ryan and Scott were informed they were supposed to monitor these lessons, hence the rule, but I can't confirm.

Instructions were amended to, find your bike, find your helmet, find a large hill, jump on, and hope you don't fall.

I believe Erin broke her wrist twice on a bike. To this day, she's the only person I know who had to wear roller skate pads and a helmet while biking.

I had, at this point, ceded my position as "older" twin to Erin, on the condition that since she was the oldest, she had to do all scary things first. It was only fair. As a result, Erin has sustained a fair amount of injuries from our agreement. At one point, our German exchange student was put in charge of teaching us to bike. I'm not sure if Marian actually knew how to bike, but that didn't stop her from placing Erin on the seat of the bike (feet did not reach the pedals) and sending her down a hill.

She immediately crashed into a tree, and Marian lost "bike instructor" duties.

Note: to all "singlet" children out there—I highly recommend getting a twin. They prove very durable and useful when testing safety concerns.

After about two years of unsuccessfully learning to bike, my parents monitored my siblings teaching us to ride bikes. We miraculously learned within a month.

Several years later, when we were all teaching Bridget how to bike, I whipped out the camcorder and interviewed her as she learned. I believe there is still a recording somewhere along these lines:

Chris: "How does it feel to learn how to bike?"
Bridget: "I'm—"
Dad (in the distance, at the lawnmower): "It's ****. Absolute ****."
Bridget: "—so...excited...Mom?"

Rule 5: No playing hide and seek without an adult

Somewhere else in this compilation I believe Erin has written her story on a game of hide & seek gone horribly wrong.

Fun fact: that is not the only time hide & seek has gone wrong in our family.

As everyone knows, sometimes you start out playing hide & seek, and then become immediately distracted.

I was only about three at the time, but on one such day, my father had left out a ladder, leaning against the 788 house. We both instantly knew the ladder would be excellent in hiding, we weren't sure how though. We tried moving it to cover us, only to be disappointed you could see us through the rungs. We then came up with the ingenious idea of using the ladder to reach the roof, where no one would think to look. Erin and I took turns daring each other to go up the different rungs. As I have mentioned before, Erin had to do anything scary first, to ensure it was safe.

At some point a sibling came along, and asked why we were hopping on and off the first two rungs. We explained the process, and as a responsible child who didn't want to get in trouble for not doing their due diligence, they explained that was probably a bad idea, since we could fall off the roof.

They then left the two of us and the ladder, for you see, they had done the bare minimum, but didn't see why they should remove us from the ladder, or the ladder from us.

They had also just inspired a new game. This game was just like hide & seek, but we wanted to scare the person who was It. We decided that one of us should jump off the ladder when the person who was It came by. To make it more impressive, we should do it from higher than we ever had before.

Cue an intense montage of us going up higher and higher....six steps....ten steps. Finally, Erin reached the top of the ladder.

Right on cue, someone came around the corner, saw two-year-old Erin at the top, with me at the bottom (ready to "catch" her). Erin made eye contact, spread her arms, and jumped.

I vividly remember Erin needing stitches on her chin as I panicked and moved out of the way. Erin tells me she remembers none of this and never had stitches as a result of falling off a ladder. I blame that on the brain damage that clearly resulted from such a fall.

We were then informed that in playing hide & seek you need to define boundaries. Such as "staying on the floor" and "no climbing". Boring rules. My Dad was growing increasingly terrified that one of us would lock ourselves in the barn or 788 house, so we also had to set timers for the rounds. If you weren't found in five minutes you had to check in. One of my favorite places to hide was in laundry baskets, in closets, and in trees.

Brett had a great idea one year to scare my parents by placing Bridget's tricycle at the bottom of the tree during hide & seek, give a yell, and rub red food dye on his head and a rock. He laid on the tricycle until the adults got close and jumped up.

We weren't allowed to play hide & seek the rest of the day.

Another time, two of my siblings got stuck in the same tree. They used the cat philosophy—they couldn't figure out how to climb down so they climbed up all the way to the top of the thirty-foot pine tree. After this incident, my Dad said we couldn't climb trees unless we knew how to climb down. He also went around the property and cut off any branches below five feet—figuring that only those that could reach the branches could climb up or down.

Erin and I just stood on each other's backs, launched one twin in the air, who would grab the branch, pull themselves up, then reach down and pull the other twin up. If Bridget was with us, each of us would grab an arm and swing her up.

To get out of the tree, we were too scared to jump, so of course we just pushed each other out. It was a solid system, until the day I pushed Bridget out at the end of a round of hide & Seek and knocked the wind out of her. She was about five, and she turned blue. I thought I had killed her, and because we weren't supposed to be outside anyway (we had snuck out when our babysitting siblings weren't looking), I realized I needed to find an adult.

I decided I couldn't grab Brett—I didn't think he would know what to do with a dead body at the age of eleven. I also thought Katie and Jen would freak out. I decided I would need to talk to Ryan or Scott. I think Erin was It, and I knew she would immediately tattle on me for sororicide.

I remember tapping Ryan on the shoulder while he played video games, and asked him to come look at an ouchie Bridget had. I figured I'd break it to him slowly that his youngest sister had died. As we turned the corner to the side yard, Bridget made a miraculous recovery. I remember thanking my lucky stars. Ryan did not question how Bridget had ended up on the ground, as blue as the sky. I'm grateful for his discretion. We brought her in, and gave her chocolate chips, and said she shouldn't mention it to Mom & Dad.

Thanks for covering up my crime, Ryan.

Rule 6: Do chores every day

I don't know if I have any stories to follow this rule. I can confirm that as an adult, this is a very useful life skill—doing some parts of your duties every day makes it so things don't pile up. It's also useful as it makes you look busy every day. I should highlight this rule also made it clear to me it's important to look productive versus be productive. Carrying a damp washcloth implies you are dusting—or putting a mop bucket in the bathroom has the implication that the floor was mopped. There are a lot of ways someone can employ productivity versus actually being productive.

I remember being frustrated that homework took so long, until one of my siblings passed on sage advice: You are allocated one hour for homework, so the less time you spend on homework, the more of that hour is "free" time. It was all about efficiency at that point. If you did your homework at school, you had free time in the evenings. Our teachers tried to stress homework was for home, but my parents weren't too interested in fighting a battle that essentially said "stop doing your homework, only do it at prescribed times". From their point of view, the homework was finished.

On that note, bringing your backpack filled with school books home implies you are doing it at home, but we all know the truth.

To the reader: I'm positive there is something you are putting off. This is your hint to go and do that task.

Rule 7: When in doubt—eat and sleep

Most situations can be resolved through working around the problem. Some situations cannot be resolved, as not all problems have solutions.

This is a lesson I learned early on, and I have actually spoken to several siblings about. When stressed, the number one thing we would do is make a sandwich, then take a nap.

The philosophy can be summarized as simply: If you encounter a problem you cannot outthink, and you are unable to change any factors, accept the only factor that will change is you and time. By eating, you recharge yourself and allow yourself to step away from the problem. Sleeping takes care of the time issues. When you return, the problem will have either resolved itself, or you are in a better position to take care of it.

This is a story about the one time in my life eating and sleeping did not fix all my problems.

I attended two high schools growing up. At the first, there was no dress code, except for the "modesty" code. Essentially, no ripped jeans, sweats, or leggings. No shirts with swear words, etc. Naturally, since 90% of my dress code reflected this (I didn't own leggings until I was sixteen), I dressed in jeans and t-shirts 90% of the time, the one exception being dress up or Mass days, where skirts/dresses were mandatory (later on an exception was made for girls to wear dress pants or khakis). I specifically chose outfits I could wear tennis shoes with, and picked the comfiest dress shoes I could find.

At my second high school, a uniform was mandatory. It was also horrifying. If you have ever been or known a teenager, they are rife with insecurity and embarrassment. The uniform only got worse as years went on. Khakis with polos were my new norm, and it was terrible. I still refuse to wear khakis to this day.

One of the few exceptions were "dress" days—days you could dress up and wear nicer clothes. I absolutely took this opportunity and purchased "power shoes". For the unfamiliar reader, power shoes are shoes that allow the wear to topple over their inferior subordinates. Some may refer to them as "high heels" or pumps. These would be the inferior subordinates. Power shoes add the extra few inches that truly show a person's dexterity and balance, even more so if you can sprint in them (a feat I used to demonstrate, even biking in my four-inchers on a dare).

My shoes got higher and higher, and most days, I had a minimum half-inch to an inch. As many of my family members will tell you, I am a plague child. My brother once told me, out of what I can only hope was love, that I was the child that would have been left to the elements. I was dropped down a flight of stairs as a baby, and had two rows of teeth for several years, I have horrible vision (I didn't know trees had individual leaves—I thought the green blobs would shatter and fall to the ground in the fall, creating the leaves I knew since I could hold them up to my face), I've caught almost every plague, being the one kid to catch swine flu in my class back in '08. I'm not a healthy person, which is hilarious, as back in high school I had a stringent diet of vegetables, seitan, and egg sandwiches, and religiously took my multivitamin.

Because this was me, I had a tiny cut on the bottom of my foot. I resolved to ignore it—after all, up to this point I had ignored most cuts, and all had healed. Each day, I would put a bandaid on my foot, (it was on the pad near the front I believe), and strap on my power shoes. Each day, it got a little worse oddly enough.

At this time, I played basketball and had a part-time job as a retail associate selling pre-teen clothing. I was on my feet for quite a bit of the day. After two or three weeks of dealing with the cut by eating and sleeping, it turned black, just slightly. I figured this was another step in the healing process and resolved to continue my course of action, which to date, had been nothing.

The cut got bigger, up to half an inch, and red outside the black. It started to throb. I took ibuprofen. This shockingly did not solve the issue. After the next week, I began to be unable to put pressure on my foot anymore and realized I may have to forego power shoes the next day.

This. Would. Not. Do.

I closed the store with my manager, limped home (it was my right foot of course, so I hit the gas and brakes with my left), and asked my Mom if Dad was home. My Mom, being a mother, knew that we only asked for Dad if it was serious, and she checked the clock, and asked if she should text him. I let her know my foot was hurting, and I just wanted him to check it before bed that night.

As it wasn't an emergency, we ate dinner and afterwards my Dad had me sit on the stairs and had me take off my sock. It revealed a swollen, red, and angry foot with a black cut. What appeared to be a vein was red and enlarged, going up to my ankle.

My Dad set my foot down, poked it. Then turned around, grabbed his coat, asked for the time, and told me not to move or I would die.

My Mom filled in this story for me, as being confronted with mortality, even if it is from an extremely pessimistic surgeon, does tend to shock as a tender teenager. My Dad jumped in the car and asked my Mom to google pharmacies and their hours (it was about 8 PM). He went to the nearest one, wrote me a prescription for antibiotics and other medications, then drove home. Before explaining anything, he made me take a slew of medications and told me I had contracted lymph poisoning, otherwise known as lymphangitis.

"If you weren't my kid, I would take you to the ER, but this way you can stay home."

He then took a permanent marker and marked several spots on my leg, which had what I now realize are the tell-tale red streaks of my lymph vessels being inflamed from infection. He marked a spot and said if it went past that point, I would need to go to the ER. Then, he told me to sleep well and go to sleep.

I shockingly did not sleep.

I was out of school for the next two days, watching tv, and texting my friends. I was not allowed to leave my bed, and had to keep my foot propped high in the air. I also slept in a loft bed, which meant that I had to get in and out without putting any pressure on my foot. My Dad returned several times the first day to poke my foot and continue the abstract drawing of my infection.

I was allowed to return to school on the third day, on the express orders to forego power shoes for a week (OR LONGER!), and to stay off my feet.

The next week in Health we covered the lymphatic system, and I learned all about my minor case of lymph poisoning.

If you or someone you love has inflamed lymph nodes, red streaks over their body, aches, and an inflamed cut, talk to your doctor about not avoiding your problems.

Rule 8: Be in an organized sport

This was a rule growing up that was heatedly debated by several members of the family. On my parents' side, they believed being in an organized sport taught you physical exercises that would keep you healthy, help you with time management, and provide social engagements outside of the wild heroin parties all eleven-year-olds get up to.

On the children's side, organized sports are a source of pure dread. At least for some. Some people genuinely enjoy the thought of having to sprint up and down a court every single day, and toss a ball back and forth. If the reader is unable to determine which side of the fence I sit on, let it be clear—you are more likely to find me in a library than on the basketball court.

I have a memory of one of my brothers telling my Dad all benefits of organized sports could be found outside of the sport. As long as he tried to meet each of those goals in a separate activity, he should be allowed to drop pursuing the sport. Much to his frustration, our high school did not "cut" from the team, meaning, no matter how terrible you were at the sport, you would always sit, even if you never played.

There are many things I learned playing basketball, volleyball, and the two years spent in track. The first is: wait to eat until after strenuous activity, unless you want to revisit your sack lunch. The next is: you will surely meet and bond with your teammates over the sport. Said bonding may include how much you dislike playing said sport.

I know several of my siblings loved playing their sportsball, to which I say, good for you! Give me a set of rollerblades or track shoes any day over a ball or bat.

Rule 9: Tell someone where you are going

I feel like this rule is obvious. As a child, my parents would share with me horror stories of being kidnapped, of kids who got lost, of the student who was locked out of their apartment and froze to death.

Whenever you are leaving to go somewhere, make sure someone knows where you are, and when you will be back. This prompts the search party for when you inevitably trip over your face down the stairs and perish tragically, so your body is found sooner than later.

It is an excellent rule, and has a second, subsidiary rule—make sure you have an alibi. It makes sense to go with someone, especially if you intend on breaking rules meant to be broken. This second person can vouch for you.

I truly believe that the pursuit of marriage and love is searching for the person who will be your alibi.

Rule 10: Make time for friends, but make time for yourself

My Mom used to have some odd rules, or so I thought, about socializing.

You don't visit someone two days in a row, especially if they entertained you. You could invite them over the next day. You also never invite yourself over to someone's home or event. You shouldn't make plans every weekend, rather, every other weekend. This ensures you can host several weekends a month, but also ensures you meet your own personal responsibilities. You should always clean before guests come over. It's rude to clean up other people's houses as well. You shouldn't hang out with someone for more than three hours unless it's a sleepover—in which case you should leave before 10 AM the next day.

As an adult, I appreciate these rules, and while I was frustrated my Mom didn't let me see my friends all the time, I totally appreciate them as an adult. Setting aside every other weekend for "me" time to do my chores and work on hobbies does wonders for my mental and emotional state. Spacing hangouts with friends allows you not to be overwhelmed and ensures your social calendar is booked without being too busy. It's a form of self-care that often gets forgotten, because if you can't be comfortable by yourself, how can you ever expect to be comfortable with others? Most of my friends now know I'm only available on certain days of the week, which I'm sure frustrates them. Unfortunately, I'm a creature of habit, but it is satisfying knowing the week ahead who I'm having coffee with, and what I'm doing Friday night. I'm the exact opposite of a "spur of the Moment" person, and without these rules my mother taught me I'm sure I would be an anxious mess.

"But Chris—" you, the reader, might say, "who's to say what you would be without those rules! Maybe you secretly love hanging out with people daily."

Take your extroverted nonsense elsewhere. These rules are guidelines, not anything hard and fast. Of course I hang out with people on a regular basis, sometimes daily. I also recognize that frankly, talking to people and being "on" socially is draining—friendships take energy to maintain. There is no point in maintaining a friendship if it is draining and harming you, and I firmly believe that you are taking advantage of a friend if you do so. Being in a mentally drained state will cause you to hurt them through action or inaction—not listening at the right Moments or being mentally present.

Self-care my people. Self-care.

20

Bridget

The Good: Mild Arson is a Family Event

Usually, lighting fires is a task done without parental permission and with a few rules. Make them small, keep them contained, and don't tell Mom, and especially do not tell Dad. These rules maintained social order in our pyromaniacs-by-boredom household. One summer, as a family, we built our biggest fire ever, and we did not follow a single one of our pre-established rules. The fire was taller than a house, contained by a ring of gasoline, and Dad was the one instigating. We were out of our comfort zone in a toasty way.

Everything from old Christmas trees, brush cleared from around the property, and random burnable junk we found in the backyard barn all went up in smoke after a few hours of intense heat. Certainly a bonfire to remember.

Well, it was less of a "bonfire" and more like a "domesticated wildfire." We found we could not get closer than seven feet to the flames or we'd risk a nice red tan. Our popcorn sadly melted in flames as the poor container couldn't keep up with the heat, and we didn't even think about whipping out the s'more's given how distanced we needed to be from the flames. A family friend remarked that he could see the flames over the treetops as he drove in from the highway.

I'll never forget hearing the sirens fly down the highway, and Dad telling us to go grab a hose, betting that the fire department would not check to see if it was attached to any spigot. And he bet correctly. Fake it 'til you make it was the lesson of the day. The fire engine rolled up and then the firemen took my Dad aside to talk about "safety" or whatever out by the engine. Meanwhile, the younger half of our family pretended that we weren't imitating fire monsters. Brett, meanwhile pulled up a seat in front of our fire to show off his "evil overlord" status.

It's a good thing Jenny documented quite a bit for her Photo of the Day project, so in case the whole area went up in flame we could remember this day fondly in a family album.

21

The Bad: Broken Wrist Blues

 I think back frequently to the winter of my first-grade year. The air was crisp, snow was falling slightly, and kids were waiting around one of the doors for their parents to bring them home. I was one such child. I was in my snow gear, ready for home, so when my friends started playing on one of the mountainous piles of snow near the school, accumulated by the snowplows, I thought it was a wonderful way to pass the time.

 Up and down we went on the snow hill. My friends and I had created a slope to slide down. Laughing and racing, it was all well and fun. Until it wasn't. I don't remember what caused me to need to stop, but I stuck my hand out to slow myself down, and something in my hand began to hurt. Naturally, I began to cry, as kids do when they are in pain and scared. I think someone found a sibling to assist somehow, and eventually Mom showed up.

 Was it distressing to not have anyone believe you that something was broken in your hand? Sure, but when one cries loud enough, is annoying, and is a constant cause of discomfort, people tend to listen to you, even if it takes some time. After many tears and screams, eventually Mom decided to humor me, and take me to Dad's office to check out my busted hand.

 As it turns out, after some examination, and a very cool X-ray, my hand was broken! Or my wrist. Some delicate bone had a greenstick fracture and would heal up pretty nicely since I was a kid. I was handed off to nurses to get a cast, which made me feel a lot better, given that now I wasn't bumping the injury constantly.

I learned a few things from this. One, never stop a fall with predominantly one hand as that is a very poor decision. Two, if you're hurt just be annoying until someone gives in and accommodates for you.

22

The Ugly: Locked in a Car

It was autumn. I was in fourth or fifth grade. I was a good sister and accompanied my family to one of Brett's football games out of town. It was a long way out of town, or at least felt like it. While I do not recall whether the football team won or lost, but I do know that I was tired from all the exciting elements of the day. So on the way back home, I rolled up into a random comforter I found in the car and fell asleep.

I woke up in the dark, still in the minivan, except I was alone. At first, I was distressed, but I decided to assess my options before I started to cry. I checked the door into the house from the garage. Locked. I walked outside, where I confirmed it was indeed, late at night. I walked to the front door, which was also locked. I then walked to the patio door, the door to the dog yard, and checked all other back doors. All locked. Eventually I went back to the garage, hopped into the driver seat and just let loose on the horn, hoping one of the many residents sleeping in the house would wake up. No success.

Eventually, I gave up on getting to my bed for the evening. It was a weekend, I didn't really need the sleep. I went outside again, explored until I got cold, then found myself back in the minivan. I climbed over Brett's smelly football gear, wrapped myself up in the comforter, and fell asleep. I figured morning would arrive eventually.

Indeed, the earth did keep turning while I was asleep. I woke up again to the sound of Mom hopping into the car, off to run some errands. Finally! A person! I think I scared her a little when I said, "Good morning!"

I was let back into the house and all was well after that. Apparently, I had scared some siblings overnight as well, with the honking and knocking on all the doors, but none were brave enough to check it out. I survived the night and that's what counts, I guess.

www.ingramcontent.com/pod-product-compliance
Lightning Source LLC
Chambersburg PA
CBHW072016290426
44109CB00018B/2256